Fruit Recipes

Meal Ideas for How to Cook with All Types of Fruits

By
BookSumo Press
All rights reserved

Published by
http://www.booksumo.com

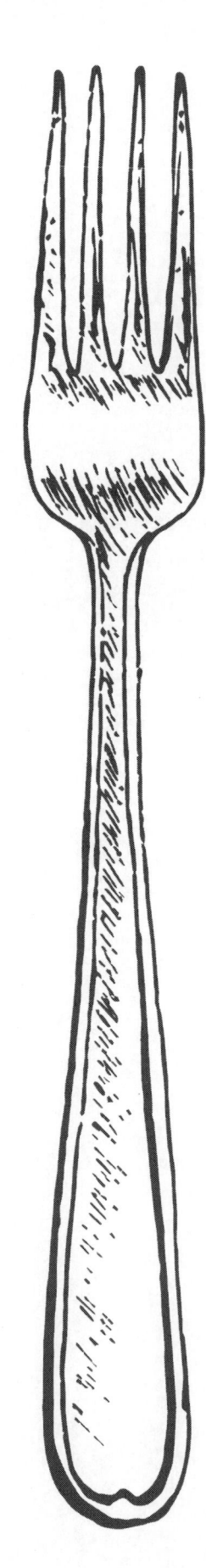

Table of Contents

North Philly Pizza 7

Sweeter Flan 8

August's Salad 10

Californian Bread 11

Manhattan Spritzer 12

Rustic Muffins 13

North Carolina Style Lemonade 14

Kansas Lemonade 15

Middle Eastern Smoothie 16

Brazilian Style Cha Cha 17

Strawberry Pavlova 18

Rice and Kiwi Curry Lunch Wrap 19

Jungle Juice 20

Kiwi Orange Chicken 21

Rain Forest Juice 22

Easy Homemade Julep 23

Southern French Cocktail 24

Jiggy Juice 25

Key Lime Time 26

Watermelon Kiwi Cake 27

Summery Quinoa Salad 28

Best-Ever Cheesecake 29

Flavorful Chicken & Rice 31

Mango Pudding American Style 32

Magnificent cheese Balls 33

5-Ingredient Mango Salmon 34

Scrumptious Mango Bars 35

4-Ingredient Mango Soup 36

Mango Curry Indian Style 37

Tastier Mango Drink 38

Fiesta Mango Salad 39

Mexican Mango Drink 40

Indian Spicy Mango Drink 41

Citrus Mango Smoothie 42

Tropical Fruit Punch 43

Mango Drink Hong Kong Style 44

Healthier Smoothie 45

Delish Mango Pie 46

Comforting Mango Cobbler 47

Luscious Fruity Dessert 48

Delightful Summer Salsa 49

Refreshing Fruity Sorbet 50

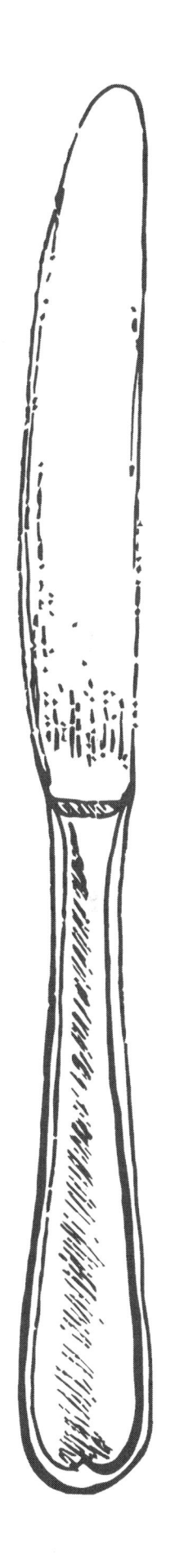

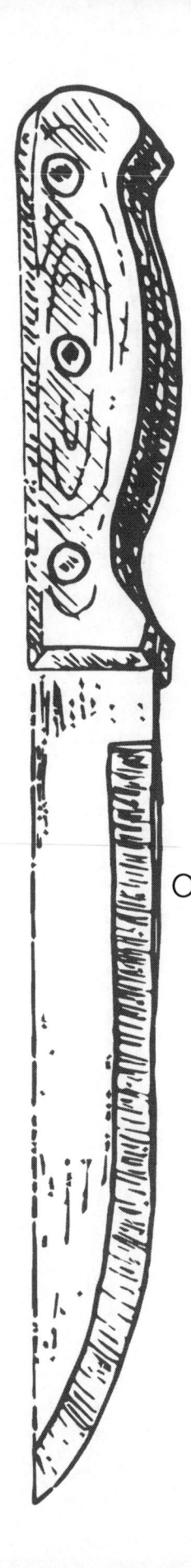

Special Peach Treat 51

Italian Peach Bruschetta 52

Refreshing Peach Salad 53

Gourmet Fall-Time Dessert 54

Tasty Chicken Polynesian Style 55

Asian Style Peach Soup 56

Deliciously Glazed Chicken 57

Chunky Fruit Chutney 58

Lancaster Strawberries 59

Greatly-Flavored Muffins 60

Fantastic Peach Bread 61

German Peach Pancakes 62

Overnight Peach French Toast Casserole 63

French Style Candy 64

Satisfying Peach Crumble 65

Delicious Fruity Tartlets 66

Homemade Asian Plum Sauce 67

Countryside Plum Crisp 68

Potato and Plum Dumplings 69

Easy Homemade Plum Cake 70

Cinnamon Clove and Plum Bread 71

German Plum Cake 72

A Very Light Flan 73

Plum Jelly 101 74

How to Make Tapioca Pudding 75

Rustic Pie 76

Moist Homemade Plum Lemon Cake 78

Traditional French Dessert 79

Jalapeno Plum Chipotle Sauce 80

Persian Inspired Cardamom and Plum Jam 82

New Age Plum Cake 83

Agave Butter 84

Fruity Plum Rolls German Style 85

Plum Poblano Salsa 86

Plum No Sugar Butter 87

Asian Inspired Chicken 88

I ♥ Strawberry Drinks 89

Strawberry Shortcake 101 90

Bread for Brunch 91

Weekend Breakfast Muffins 92

John the Juice Smoothie 93

Alternative Jam 94

Northern California Lemonade 95

5-Ingredient Cinnamon Strawberry Crisp 96

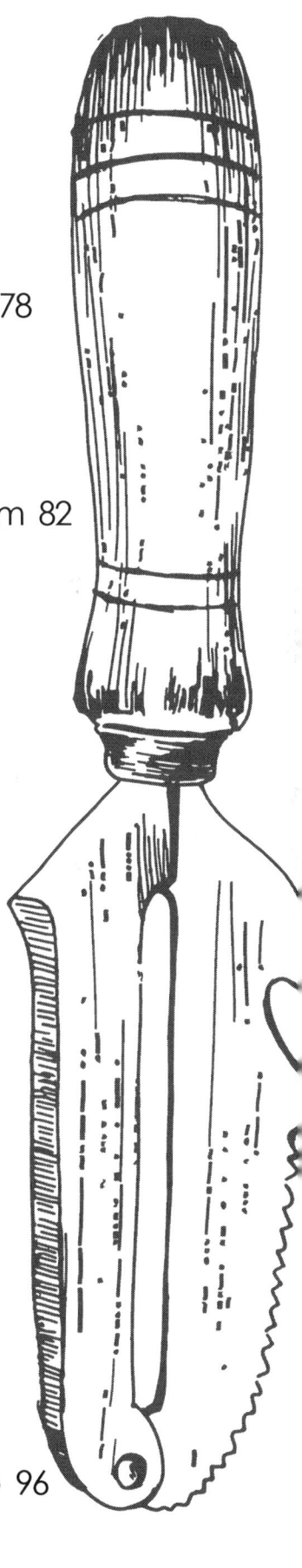

Perfect Strawberry Topping 97

Zanzibar Pie 98

Lunch Box Salad 99

Artisanal Syrup 100

Fruity Nachos 101

Mediterranean Strawberries 102

Strawberry Smoothie Bowl 103

Spring Sorbet 101 104

North Philly Pizza

🥣 Prep Time: 15 mins
⏲ Total Time: 2 hrs 59 mins

Servings per Recipe: 12
Calories	283 kcal
Fat	15.4 g
Carbohydrates	35.6 g
Protein	3 g
Cholesterol	25 mg
Sodium	218 mg

Ingredients

- 1 (16.5 oz.) package refrigerated sliceable sugar cookies, sliced
- 1 (8 oz.) package Cream Cheese, softened
- 1/4 C. sugar
- 1/2 tsp vanilla
- 1 tbsp water
- 4 C. assorted cut-up fruit (kiwi, strawberries, blueberries, drained canned mandarin oranges)
- 1/4 C. apricot preserves, pressed through sieve to remove lumps

Directions

1. Set your oven to 375 degrees F before doing anything else and line a 12-inch pizza pan with the foil paper.
2. Place the cookie dough slices in the pizza pan in a single layer and press together to form a crust.
3. Cook in the oven for about 14 minutes.
4. Remove from the oven and keep aside to cool completely.
5. Invert the crust onto a plate and carefully remove the foil.
6. Then, turn the crust over.
7. In a bowl, add the cream cheese, sugar and vanilla and beat till well combined.
8. Spread the cream cheese mixture over the crust and top with the fruit.
9. In a bowl, mix together the preserves and water.
10. Coat the fruit with the preserve mixture and refrigerate for about 2 hours.

SWEETER
Flan

🥣 Prep Time: 30 mins
🕐 Total Time: 1 hr 42 mins

Servings per Recipe: 12
Calories   430 kcal
Fat   24.2 g
Carbohydrates   50.1g
Protein   4.9 g
Cholesterol   56 mg
Sodium   170 mg

Ingredients

Crust:
2 1/8 C. all-purpose flour
1/2 tsp cream of tartar
1/2 tsp baking soda
1/2 C. white sugar
1/2 C. confectioners' sugar
1/2 C. butter
1/2 C. vegetable oil
1 egg
1/2 tsp vanilla extract
Filling:
1 (8 oz.) package cream cheese, softened
1/3 C. white sugar
1/2 tsp vanilla extract
Fruit:
3 C. fresh strawberries, hulled and halved
1 C. fresh blueberries, rinsed and dried
3 kiwifruit, peeled and thinly sliced
Glaze:
1 tbsp cornstarch
1/4 C. white sugar
1/2 C. water
1/2 C. orange juice
2 tbsp lemon juice

Directions

1. Set your oven to 350 degrees F before doing anything else and grease a 15x10-inch jelly roll pan.
2. For crust in a bowl, sift together the flour, cream of tartar and baking soda.
3. In another bowl, add the white and confectioners' sugars, butter, vegetable oil, egg, and vanilla and beat till creamy.
4. Add the flour mixture and mix till well combined.
5. In the bottom of the prepared pan, place the dough evenly.
6. Cook in the oven for about 10-12 minutes.
7. Remove from the oven and keep aside to cool completely.
8. For filling in a bowl, add the cream cheese, sugar and vanilla and beat till creamy.

9. Place the filling mixture over the cooled crust.
10. Arrange the fruit over the filling and refrigerate.
11. For the glaze in a small pan, mix together the sugar and cornstarch on medium heat.
12. Add the water, orange juice and lemon juice and beat to combine.
13. Bring to a boil for about 1 minute.
14. Remove from the heat and keep aside to cool completely.
15. Pour the glaze over the fruit evenly and refrigerate before serving.

AUGUST'S Salad

🥣 Prep Time: 30 mins
🕒 Total Time: 30 mins

Servings per Recipe: 12
Calories   126 kcal
Fat   1.4 g
Carbohydrates   25.5g
Protein   4.7 g
Cholesterol   4 mg
Sodium   56 mg

Ingredients

1 (16 oz.) package fresh strawberries, hulled and halved
1 large peach, pitted and cut into bite-size pieces
2 plums, pitted and cut into bite-size pieces
2 kiwi fruit, peeled and cut into bite-size pieces
1 C. dark sweet cherries, pitted and halved
1 C. honeydew melon balls or cubes
1 C. cantaloupe cubes
1 C. cubed fresh pineapple
1 C. grapes
2 (16 oz.) containers low-fat vanilla yogurt

Directions

1. In a large salad bowl, mix together the strawberries, peach, plums, kiwi fruit, cherries, honeydew melon, cantaloupe, pineapple and grapes.
2. Serve with a topping of the yogurt.

Californian Bread

🥣 Prep Time: 15 mins
🕐 Total Time: 1 hr 15 mins

Servings per Recipe: 10
Calories   249.5
Fat   10.5g
Cholesterol   61.6mg
Sodium   280.4mg
Carbohydrates   35.2g
Protein   4.1g

Ingredients

2 C. all-purpose flour
1 tsp baking powder
1/4 tsp baking soda
1/2 tsp salt
1/2 C. butter (soften)
2/3 C. sugar
2 eggs

1 C. peeled mashed kiwi fruit (ripe)

Directions

1. Set your oven to 350 degrees F before doing anything else and grease a 9x5x3-inch loaf pan.
2. In a bowl, sift together the flour, baking powder, baking soda and salt.
3. In another large bowl, add the butter and sugar and beat till light and fluffy.
4. Add the eggs, one at a time and beat till well combined.
5. Stir in the mashed kiwis.
6. Add the flour mixture and mix till just moistened.
7. Transfer the mixture into the prepared loaf pan.
8. Cook in the oven for about 55-65 minutes or till a toothpick inserted in the center comes out clean.
9. Remove from the oven and cool for about 10 minutes on wire rack.
10. Remove from pan and cool completely on rack.

MANHATTAN
Spritzer

🍲 Prep Time: 5 mins
🕐 Total Time: 7 mins

Servings per Recipe: 4
Calories   330.6
Fat   1.1g
Cholesterol   0.0mg
Sodium   26.3mg
Carbohydrates   83.4g
Protein   1.1g

Ingredients

4 kiwi fruits, peeled
1 (12 oz.) cans frozen lemonade concentrate, thawed

3 C. carbonated lemon-lime beverage, chilled

Directions

1. Cut the kiwi into chunks.
2. In a food processor, add the fruit chunks and lemonade concentrate and pulse till smooth.
3. Through a wire mesh strainer, strain the mixture into a pitcher, discarding solids.
4. Stir in the lemon lime drink just before serving.

Rustic Muffins

🥣 Prep Time: 30 mins
⏲ Total Time: 1 hr

Servings per Recipe: 1
Calories   219.5
Fat   5.8g
Cholesterol   31.0mg
Sodium   552.3mg
Carbohydrates   37.5g
Protein   4.6g

Ingredients

2 eggs
1/2 C. sugar
1/4 C. oil
4 large very ripe kiwi, mashed
1/4 tsp vanilla
1 tbsp lemon juice
3 C. flour

1 1/2 tsp salt
3 tsp baking powder
1 1/2 tsp baking soda

Directions

1. Set your oven to 350 degrees F before doing anything else and lightly, grease 12 cups of a muffin pan.
2. In a bowl, add the eggs, sugar and oil and beat till well combined.
3. Add the kiwi, vanilla and lemon juice and beat till well combined.
4. In another large bowl, mix together the flour, salt, baking powder and baking soda.
5. Add the kiwi mixture and mix till well combined.
6. Transfer the mixture into the prepared muffin cups evenly.
7. Cook in the oven for about 25-30 minutes or till a toothpick inserted in the center comes out clean.

NORTH CAROLINA STYLE
Lemonade

🥣 Prep Time: 5 mins
🕐 Total Time: 5 mins

Servings per Recipe: 1
Calories   98.1
Fat   0.4g
Cholesterol   31.0mg
Sodium   552.3mg
Carbohydrates   37.5g
Protein   4.6g

Ingredients

1/2 kiwi
3 medium strawberries
1 lemon
1/2 C. water

1 - 1 1/2 tbsp sugar
2 ice cubes (optional)

Directions

1. In a bowl, squeeze the kiwi and strawberries.
2. With a lemon squeezer, squeeze the lemons.
3. Add 1/2 C. of the water and sugar and stir to combine.

Kansas Lemonade

🥣 Prep Time: 30 mins
🕐 Total Time: 30 mins

Servings per Recipe: 6
Calories 171.4
Fat 0.1g
Cholesterol 0.0mg
Sodium 5.3mg
Carbohydrates 45.2g
Protein 0.4g

Ingredients

1 C. lemon juice
1 C. sugar
1 1/2 C. strawberries, washed and hulled

2 tbsp light corn syrup
Water, to fill 2 quart pitcher

Directions

1. In a blender, add the strawberries and corn syrup and pulse till smooth.
2. Through a fine sieve, strain the strawberry puree and discard the pulp and seeds.
3. In a 2 quart pitcher, add the strawberry puree, lemon juice and sugar and mix till the sugar is dissolved.
4. In serving glasses, place the ice.
5. Pour the lemonade over the ice and serve.

MIDDLE EASTERN
Smoothie

🥣 Prep Time: 3 mins
🕐 Total Time: 8 mins

Servings per Recipe: 1
Calories   323.0
Fat   1.6g
Cholesterol   0.0mg
Sodium   7.2mg
Carbohydrates   81.9g
Protein   4.3g

Ingredients

2 ripe kiwi fruits, peeled
1 large banana, frozen
3 honey dates

2/3 C. blueberries

Directions

1. In a bowl, add the dates and pour the boiling water over them.
2. Soak for about 5-10 minutes to soften.
3. Drain the dates and transfer the dates in a blender with remaining Ingredients and pulse till smooth.

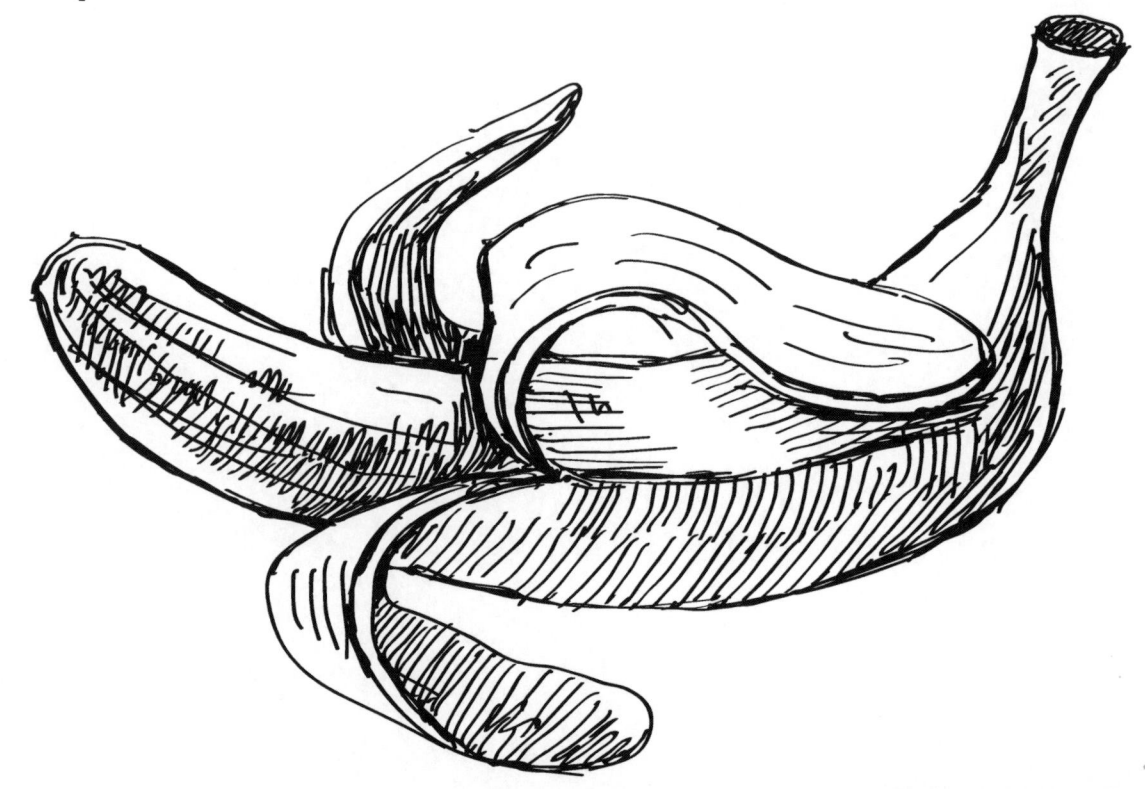

Brazilian Style Cha Cha

Prep Time: 2 mins
Total Time: 4 mins

Servings per Recipe: 1
Calories	186.4
Fat	0.2g
Cholesterol	0.0mg
Sodium	1.9mg
Carbohydrates	15.6g
Protein	0.5g

Ingredients

1/2 lime, large cut into 4 pieces
2 tsp sugar
1/3 kiwi fruit, peeled and cut into 6 chunks
2 oz. Pina colada
GARNISH
1 slice kiwi fruit

Directions

1. In a cocktail shaker, mix together the lime pieces and sugar and press with a muddler to release the juice.
2. Add the kiwifruit and press with muddler to crush.
3. Fill the shaker with the ice and measure in the Pina colada.
4. Cap the shaker and shake vigorously.
5. Pour into and old-fashioned glass and serve with a garnishing of the kiwifruit slice.

STRAWBERRY
Pavlova

🥣 Prep Time: 30 mins
🕒 Total Time: 2 hrs

Servings per Recipe: 8
Calories   308.8
Fat   22.2g
Cholesterol   81.5mg
Sodium   44.1mg
Carbohydrates   26.1g
Protein   3.0g

Ingredients

3 egg whites
1 pinch cream of tartar
3/4 C. granulated sugar
1 tsp vanilla

2 C. whipping cream
4 C. strawberries, sliced

Directions

1. Set your oven to 275 degrees F before doing anything else and line a baking sheet with a piece of foil.
2. In a large bowl, add the egg whites and cream of tartar and beat till soft peaks form.
3. Add the sugar, 1 tbsp at a time and beat till glossy peaks form.
4. Add the vanilla and beat till well combined.
5. Place the meringue onto the prepared baking sheet into a 10-inch circle, pushing up the edges to form a slight ridge.
6. Cook in the oven for about 1 1/2 hours.
7. Turn off the oven but leave the meringue in the oven to dry completely.
8. Remove from the oven.
9. Carefully, remove the foil and keep aside to cool completely.
10. Arrange the meringue onto a serving platter.
11. Spread the whipped cream over the meringue and top with the strawberries.
12. Cut into the wedges and serve.

Rice and Kiwi Curry Lunch Wrap

Prep Time: 10 mins
Total Time: 10 mins

Servings per Recipe: 1
Calories 1008.5
Fat 30.9g
Cholesterol 0.0mg
Sodium 21.5mg
Carbohydrates 176.1g
Protein 14.4g

Ingredients

2 tbsp lime juice
1 garlic clove, minced
2 tbsp olive oil
1 tsp curry powder
1 jalapeno pepper, minced
1 tsp cumin
1 tsp honey
1/4 C. purple onion, chopped
6 kiwi fruits, pureed
1 3/4 C. cooked rice
cream cheese
tortilla

Directions

1. In a bowl, add all the Ingredients except the rice and mix till well combined.
2. In a large bowl, add the rice and chutney gently, stir to combine.
3. Refrigerate for about an hour.
4. Spread about 1 tbsp of the cream cheese on a tortilla and top with about 1/4 C. of the rice mixture and roll up.
5. You can also use this chutney to marinade chicken or fish.

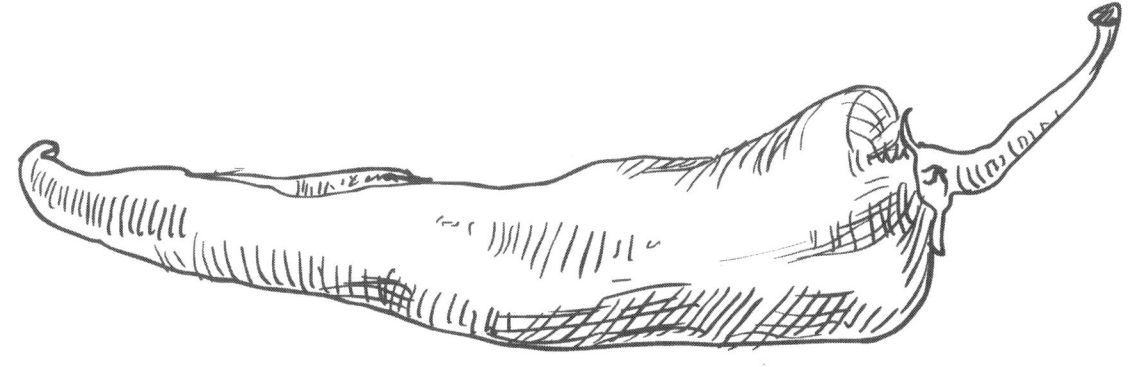

JUNGLE
Juice

🥣 Prep Time: 10 mins
🕒 Total Time: 10 mins

Servings per Recipe: 1
Calories   1923.3
Fat   3.9g
Cholesterol   0.0mg
Sodium   24.1mg
Carbohydrates   488.5g
Protein   8.7g

Ingredients

3 kiwi fruits, peeled and halved (cut of one slice for garnish)
7 oz. grapes, washed
3 -5 grapes (to garnish)

Directions

1. Extract the juice of kiwi through the juicer, followed by the grapes.
2. Transfer the juice into a glass and serve with a garnishing of some grapes and a kiwi slice skewered on a wooden stick.

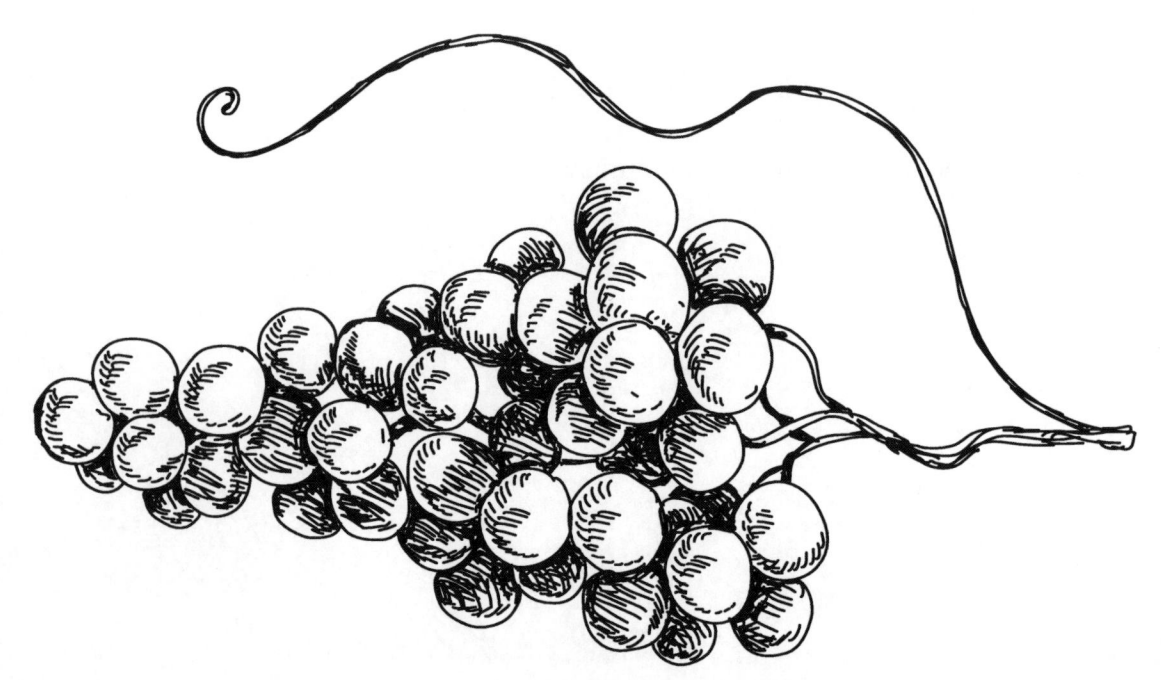

Kiwi Orange Chicken

🥣 Prep Time: 10 mins
🕐 Total Time: 1 hr

Servings per Recipe: 4
Calories   288.1
Fat   6.3g
Cholesterol   76.0mg
Sodium   928.5mg
Carbohydrates   25.4g
Protein   34.0g

Ingredients

4 C. chicken broth
4 boneless skinless chicken breasts
1 stalk celery, chopped
1 leek, white part only, chopped
4 kiwi fruits, peeled, cut into 1/4-inch slices
1 orange, washed, dried
1 lemon
1 tbsp unsalted butter

1 tbsp granulated sugar
1/8 tsp salt
1/8 tsp cayenne pepper

Directions

1. In large pan, add the chicken broth and bring to a boil.
2. Add the chicken breasts and simmer for about 10 minutes, skimming off fat from the top.
3. Add the celery and leek and simmer for about 10 minutes.
4. Remove the chicken from broth and keep aside, covered.
5. In a serving dish, arrange the kiwifruit in a fan-shaped pattern.
6. Sprinkle the half of the orange zest over the kiwifruit.
7. In a small bowl, extract the juice of orange and lemon.
8. In a small pan, melt the butter and cook the sugar for about 5 minutes, stirring continuously.
9. Add the orange and lemon juices and stir till well combined.
10. Boil till the sauce is reduced to about 2 tbsp.
11. Stir in the salt and cayenne pepper.
12. Cut the chicken breasts into thin strips and arrange over the kiwifruit.
13. Serve with a topping of the sauce.

RAIN FOREST
Juice

🥣 Prep Time: 5 mins
🕐 Total Time: 5 mins

Servings per Recipe: 1
Calories   211.3
Fat   1.1g
Cholesterol   0.0mg
Sodium   10.8mg
Carbohydrates   53.0g
Protein   14.4g

Ingredients

1/2 C. mint leaf
2 kiwi, unpeeled
8 oz. fresh pineapple, unpeeled

1/2 lime juice

Directions

1. Extract the juice of the mint, kiwi and pineapple through the hopper.
2. Transfer the juice into a serving glass.
3. Add the lime juice and stir to combine.
4. Serve immediately.

Easy Homemade Julep

Prep Time: 15 mins
Total Time: 20 mins

Servings per Recipe: 2
Calories	189.9
Fat	0.6g
Cholesterol	0.0mg
Sodium	11.0mg
Carbohydrates	47.3g
Protein	1.4g

Ingredients

- 3 tbsp sugar
- 1/2 C. hot water
- 2 C. ice
- 3 kiwi fruits, peeled
- 2 tbsp frozen limeade concentrate
- 2 tbsp chopped of fresh mint
- 3 oz. Bourbon (optional)

Directions

1. In a bowl add the hot water and sugar and stir to dissolve completely.
2. Keep aside to cool slightly.
3. In a blender, add the ice, kiwis, limeade, mint, the sugar mixture and bourbon and pulse till smooth.
4. Serve immediately.

SOUTHERN FRENCH
Cocktail

Prep Time: 15 mins
Total Time: 15 mins

Servings per Recipe: 4
Calories   154.1
Fat   0.4g
Cholesterol   0.0mg
Sodium   7.5mg
Carbohydrates   20.7g
Protein   1.1g

Ingredients

200 g strawberries, hulled and quartered
2 kiwi fruits, small, peeled and quartered
1 mango
2 (200 ml) liters lemon lime soda

Directions

1. In a food processor, add the strawberries, kiwifruit and mango and pulse till smooth.
2. In a serving jug, add the fruit mixture with the soda and stir to combine.
3. Keep aside for about 2-3 minutes to allow the bubbles to subside.
4. Divide into the cocktail evenly and serve immediately.

Jiggy Juice

Prep Time: 20 mins
Total Time: 20 mins

Servings per Recipe: 2
Calories   189.9
Fat   0.6g
Cholesterol   0.0mg
Sodium   11.0mg
Carbohydrates   47.3g
Protein   1.4g

Ingredients

7 ice cubes
2 kiwi fruits
1/3 C. orange juice
2 tbsp powdered sugar
2 tbsp granulated sugar

Directions

1. In a blender, add all the Ingredients and pulse for about 3 minutes.

KEY LIME
Time

🥣 Prep Time: 5 mins
🕐 Total Time: 5 mins

Servings per Recipe: 2
Calories   454.7
Fat   22.1g
Cholesterol   39.0mg
Sodium   149.3mg
Carbohydrates   56.9g
Protein   12.5g

Ingredients

1 C. frozen pineapple chunks
1 (6 oz.) containers key lime yogurt
1/2 C. canned unsweetened coconut milk
1 kiwi, peeled and sliced
1 tbsp honey

Directions

1. In a blender, add all the Ingredients and pulse till smooth.
2. Divide the mixture into 2 glasses and serve with a garnishing of the extra kiwi and pineapple chunks.

Watermelon Kiwi Cake

Prep Time: 20 mins
Total Time: 55 mins

Servings per Recipe: 1
Calories	5456.0
Fat	243.0g
Cholesterol	493.5mg
Sodium	5532.1mg
Carbohydrates	776.2g
Protein	62.7g

Ingredients

CAKE
1 (18 1/2 oz.) packages white cake mix
1 1/3 C. seedless watermelon, cubed
1 (4 oz.) packages strawberry kiwi gelatin powder
3 egg whites
1 tbsp vegetable oil
FROSTING
1/4 C. watermelon juice
1/2 C. butter
2 C. powdered sugar
1 (8 oz.) packages cream cheese, softened

Directions

1. Set your oven to 350 degrees F before doing anything else and grease and flour a bundt pan.
2. In a large bowl, add the dry cake mix, watermelon, gelatin powder, egg whites and oil and beat on high speed till smooth.
3. Transfer the mixture into the prepared pan.
4. Cook in the oven for about 35 minutes or till a toothpick inserted in the center comes out clean.
5. Remove from the oven and cool on a wire rack.
6. For frosting in a bowl, add the cream cheese and butter and beat till fluffy.
7. Add the sugar and watermelon juice and with a spatula, fold till well combined.
8. Frost the cake with the watermelon frosting.
9. Serve with a garnishing of the kiwi slices.

SUMMERY
Quinoa Salad

🥣 Prep Time: 10 mins
🕐 Total Time: 1 hr 25 mins

Servings per Recipe: 4
Calories   162 kcal
Fat   2.4 g
Carbohydrates   31.1g
Protein   5.3 g
Cholesterol   1 mg
Sodium   553 mg

Ingredients

1 1/2 C. chicken stock
3/4 C. quinoa
1 1/2 tsp curry powder
1/4 tsp garlic powder
1/2 tsp salt
1/4 tsp black pepper
1 mango - peeled, seeded and diced
3 green onions, chopped

Directions

1. In a pan, mix together the chicken broth, quinoa, curry powder, garlic powder, salt, and black pepper and bring to a boil on high heat.
2. Reduce the heat to medium-low and simmer, covered until for about 15-20 minutes.
3. Transfer the quinoa into a shallow dish and keep aside to cool.
4. Stir in the mango and green onions and serve.

Best-Ever Cheesecake

🥣 Prep Time: 35 mins
🕐 Total Time: 9 hrs 30 mins

Servings per Recipe: 8
Calories   468 kcal
Fat   31.6 g
Carbohydrates   38.4g
Protein   9.4 g
Cholesterol   131 mg
Sodium   311 mg

Ingredients

3/4 C. sweetened flaked coconut
3/4 C. crushed gingersnap cookies
3 tbsp melted butter
2 (8 oz.) packages cream cheese, softened
1 (10 oz.) can sweetened condensed milk
2 eggs
1 tbsp lime zest
2 tbsp lime juice
1 tbsp coconut extract
2 C. cubed fresh mango
1 tsp white sugar

Directions

1. Set your oven to 325 degrees F before doing anything else and lightly, grease a 9-inch spring form pan.
2. Transfer the mixture into the bottom and slightly up the sides of the prepared pan.
3. Cook everything in the oven for about 10 minutes.
4. Remove everything from the oven and keep aside to cool.
5. Now, set your oven to 300 degrees F.
6. In a bowl, add the softened cream cheese and beat till smooth.
7. With beater set to medium-low, slowly add the condensed milk into the bowl, mixing till well combined.
8. Add the eggs, one at a time, beating continuously till well combined.
9. Transfer about half of the cream cheese mixture into another bowl.
10. Add the lime juice and lime zest into the portion in another bowl and place the mixture over the crust evenly.
11. Stir the coconut extract in the remaining cream cheese mixture and place over the lime-flavored batter cream cheese mixture evenly.
12. Cook everything in the oven for about 45 minutes.
13. Turn the heat of the oven off, but keep the cheesecake inside with oven door

slightly open till the oven cools completely.
14. Refrigerate the cheesecake till chilled completely.
15. For mango coulis in a blender, add the mango and sugar and pulse till smooth.
16. Drizzle over cheesecake just before serving.

Flavorful Chicken & Rice

🥣 Prep Time: 15 mins
🕐 Total Time: 45 mins

Servings per Recipe: 4
Calories   379 kcal
Fat   3 g
Carbohydrates   53.8g
Protein   27.1 g
Cholesterol   61 mg
Sodium   347 mg

Ingredients

1 tsp curry powder
1/2 tsp salt
1/4 tsp black pepper
4 skinless, boneless chicken breast halves
1 C. chicken broth
1/2 C. water
1/2 C. broth

1 C. long-grain white rice
1 tbsp brown sugar
1 tbsp dried parsley
1 C. diced mango

Directions

1. In a bowl, mix together the curry powder, 1/4 tsp of the salt and black pepper.
2. Add the chicken pieces and coat with the mixture generously.
3. In a nonstick skillet, mix together the rice, broth, broth and water.
4. Stir in the remaining 1/4 tsp of the salt and all the ingredients and place the chicken pieces on the top, then bring to a boil.
5. Reduce the heat to low and simmer, covered for about 20-25 minutes.
6. Remove everything from the heat and keep aside covered for about 5 minutes before serving.

MANGO PUDDING
American Style

🥣 Prep Time: 15 mins
🕐 Total Time: 1 hr

Servings per Recipe: 8
Calories   194 kcal
Fat   6.7 g
Carbohydrates   27.9 g
Protein   6.1 g
Cholesterol   82 mg
Sodium   201 mg

Ingredients

6 slices white bread, torn into small pieces
2 mangos - peeled, seeded and diced
1/4 C. white sugar
3 eggs, lightly beaten
2 C. milk
1 1/2 tsp vanilla extract
1 1/2 tsp ground cardamom
2 tbsp butter

Directions

1. Set your oven to 350 degrees F before doing anything else and grease an 11x9-inch baking dish.
2. In a bowl, add the mango and bread pieces and toss to coat and transfer into the prepared baking dish.
3. In a bowl, add the milk, eggs, sugar, cardamom and vanilla and beat till well combined.
4. Place the egg mixture over the mango mixture and cook everything in the oven for about 45-50 minutes.

Magnificent Cheese Balls

 Prep Time: 15 mins
 Total Time: 3 hrs 15 mins

Servings per Recipe: 6
Calories   465 kcal
Fat   28.5 g
Cholesterol   47.9g
Sodium   9.6 g
Carbohydrates   71 mg
Protein   854 mg

Ingredients

11 oz. cream cheese, at room temperature
1 C. golden raisins
1 (2.1 oz.) package cooked turkey
bacon, diced
1 bunch green onions, chopped
3 tbsp sour cream
1 (9 oz.) jar mango chutney

Directions

1. In a bowl, add the cream cheese, sour cream, bacon, raisins and green onions and mix till well combined.
2. Make a ball from the mixture and cover with a plastic wrap.
3. Refrigerate for at least 3 hours or overnight before serving.
4. Place the cheese ball on a serving platter and top with the mango chutney.
5. Serve alongside the crackers for dipping.

5-INGREDIENT
Mango Salmon

🥣 Prep Time: 15 mins
🕐 Total Time: 45 mins

Servings per Recipe: 4
Calories   438 kcal
Fat   28.2 g
Carbohydrates   17.7g
Protein   29 g
Cholesterol   98 mg
Sodium   255 mg

Ingredients

2 tbsp olive oil
4 (4 oz.) fillets salmon
4 oz. Brie cheese, sliced
1 tsp butter
2 mangos - peeled, seeded, and diced

Directions

1. Set your oven to 350 degrees F before doing anything else.
2. In a large oven proof skillet, heat the oil on medium-high heat and sear the salmon for about 4 minutes per side.
3. Place the cheese over the salmon fillets evenly.
4. Cover the skillet and transfer into the oven.
5. Cook everything in the oven for about 15 minutes.
6. Meanwhile in a pan, melt the butter on medium heat and cook the mangoes for about 15 minutes.
7. Serve the salmon with a topping of the cooked mango.

Scrumptious Mango Bars

Prep Time: 15 mins
Total Time: 1 hr 30 mins

Servings per Recipe: 20
Calories	247 kcal
Fat	14.1 g
Carbohydrates	28.8g
Protein	2.4 g
Cholesterol	37 mg
Sodium	99 mg

Ingredients

1 1/2 C. butter
1/2 C. white sugar
3 C. sifted all-purpose flour
4 C. sliced mango
1/4 C. white sugar
1/4 C. all-purpose flour

1 1/2 tsp ground cinnamon
1 pinch ground allspice

Directions

1. Set your oven to 350 degrees F before doing anything else.
2. In a large bowl, add the 1/2 C. of the sugar and butter and beat till creamy.
3. Add the 3 C. of the flour and mix till well combined.
4. In the bottom of a 13x9-inch baking dish, place half of of the flour mixture and press to smooth.
5. In another bowl, mix together the remaining ingredients and place over the flour mixture evenly.
6. Top with the remaining flour mixture and cook everything in the oven for about 1 hour.

4-INGREDIENT
Mango Soup

🍲 Prep Time: 10 mins
🕐 Total Time: 10 mins

Servings per Recipe: 3
Calories   319 kcal
Fat   14.4 g
Cholesterol   49.2g
Sodium   4.7 g
Carbohydrates   45 mg
Protein   53 mg

Ingredients

2 mango - peeled, seeded, and cubed
1/4 C. white sugar
1 lemon, zested and juiced
1 1/2 C. half-and-half

Directions

1. In a blender, add all the ingredients and pulse till smooth.
2. Serve chilled.

Mango Curry
Indian Style

Prep Time: 25 mins
Total Time: 45 mins

Servings per Recipe: 4
Calories	323 kcal
Fat	21.6 g
Carbohydrates	19.1g
Protein	17.7 g
Cholesterol	0 mg
Sodium	175 mg

Ingredients

1 tbsp sesame oil
5 cloves garlic, minced
1 tbsp minced ginger
1 firm mango, peeled and sliced
3 tbsp yellow curry powder
2 tbsp chopped cilantro

1 (14 oz.) can light coconut milk
1 (14 oz.) package extra firm tofu, cubed
1/4 tsp salt and pepper to taste

Directions

1. In a large skillet, heat the oil on medium-high heat and sauté the ginger and garlic for about 1-2 minutes.
2. Add the mango and cook for about 1 minute.
3. Stir in the cilantro and curry powder and cook for about 1 minute.
4. Stir in the coconut milk and bring to a simmer.
5. Stir in the tofu, salt and black pepper and simmer, stirring occasionally for about 5 minutes.

TASTIER
Mango Drink

🥣 Prep Time: 5 mins
🕐 Total Time: 5 mins

Servings per Recipe: 4
Calories 121 kcal
Fat 1.2 g
Cholesterol 27.8g
Sodium 2.3 g
Carbohydrates 3 mg
Protein 50 mg

Ingredients

2 (15.25 oz.) cans mango pulp, or mango slices with juice
1/2 C. plain yogurt
1/4 C. milk

2 C. ice cubes

Directions

1. In a blender, add all the ingredients and pulse till smooth.

Fiesta Mango Salad

Prep Time: 20 mins
Total Time: 40 mins

Servings per Recipe: 8
Calories	81 kcal
Fat	5 g
Cholesterol	9.1g
Sodium	1.8 g
Carbohydrates	0 mg
Protein	7 mg

Ingredients

4 C. shredded cabbage
1/2 C. finely chopped red onion
1 fresh mango, cubed
1/2 C. walnut pieces

1/4 C. SPLENDA(R) Granular
3/4 C. white rice vinegar

Directions

1. In a bowl, mix together the cabbage, mango, onion and walnut.
2. In another small bowl, mix together the Splenda and vinegar.
3. Pour over the salad and toss to coat well.
4. Serve immediately or it can be served chilled too.

MEXICAN
Mango Drink

🥣 Prep Time: 10 mins
🕐 Total Time: 10 mins

Servings per Recipe: 2
Calories   255 kcal
Fat   3.9 g
Cholesterol   52.1g
Sodium   6.7 g
Carbohydrates   15 mg
Protein   82 mg

Ingredients

1 mango - peeled, seeded and diced
1 1/2 C. milk
3 tbsp honey
1 C. ice cubes

Directions

1. In a blender, add all the ingredients and pulse till smooth.
2. Serve immediately.

Indian
Spicy Mango Drink

🥣 Prep Time: 15 mins
🕐 Total Time: 15 mins

Servings per Recipe: 3
Calories   228 kcal
Fat   3 g
Cholesterol   43.6 g
Sodium   9.4 g
Carbohydrates   10 mg
Protein   121 mg

Ingredients

1 large mango - peeled, seeded, and diced
3 tbsp brown sugar
2 tbsp chopped fresh mint
1 tsp freshly ground star anise
1 tsp freshly ground cardamom
1 tbsp lime juice
2 C. plain yogurt
3 sprigs fresh mint for garnish

Directions

1. In a blender, add all the ingredients except the mint and pulse till smooth.
2. Transfer into the glasses and serve with a garnishing of the mint leaves.

CITRUS
Mango Smoothie

🥣 Prep Time: 5 mins
🕐 Total Time: 5 mins

Servings per Recipe: 4
Calories   150 kcal
Fat   0.6 g
Cholesterol   38.4g
Sodium   1.3 g
Carbohydrates   0 mg
Protein   9 mg

Ingredients

3 C. diced mango
1 1/2 C. chopped fresh or frozen peaches
1/4 C. chopped orange segments
1/4 C. chopped and pitted nectarine
1/2 C. orange juice
2 C. ice

Directions

1. In a blender, add all the ingredients and pulse till smooth.

Tropical Fruit Punch

🥣 Prep Time: 10 mins
🕐 Total Time: 10 mins

Servings per Recipe: 8
Calories	61 kcal
Fat	0.1 g
Cholesterol	15.4g
Sodium	0.5 g
Carbohydrates	0 mg
Protein	5 mg

Ingredients

1 C. sliced mango
1 C. diced, peeled papaya
1 C. orange juice
1/4 C. lime juice

1/4 C. white sugar, or to taste
1 tsp grated orange zest
4 C. water

Directions

1. In a blender, add the papaya and mango and pulse till smooth.
2. Add the remaining ingredients and pulse till well combined.
3. Serve immediately over the crushed ice.

MANGO DRINK
Hong Kong Style

- Prep Time: 10 mins
- Total Time: 50 mins

Servings per Recipe: 2
Calories   315 kcal
Fat   12.3 g
Carbohydrates   52.9 g
Protein   1.7 g
Cholesterol   0 mg
Sodium   14 mg

Ingredients

1/2 C. small pearl tapioca
1 mango - peeled, seeded and diced
14 ice cubes

1/2 C. coconut milk

Directions

1. In a pan of boiling water, cook the tapioca pearls for about 10 minutes, stirring occasionally.
2. Cover and remove everything from the heat, then keep aside for about 30 minutes.
3. Drain well and refrigerate, covered before serving.
4. In a blender, add the mango and ice and pulse till smooth.
5. Divide the chilled tapioca pearls in 2 tall glasses and top with the mango mixture, followed by the coconut milk.

Healthier Smoothie

Prep Time: 10 mins
Total Time: 10 mins

Servings per Recipe: 2
Calories   198 kcal
Fat   0.4 g
Cholesterol   47.5g
Sodium   4.7 g
Carbohydrates   2 mg
Protein   58 mg

Ingredients

- 1 mango - peeled, seeded and cubed
- 1 tbsp white sugar
- 2 tbsp honey
- 1 C. nonfat milk
- 1 tsp lemon juice
- 1 C. ice cubes

Directions

1. In a blender, add all the ingredients and pulse till smooth.
2. Divide the ice cubes in two serving glasses.
3. Add the mango smoothie over ice and serve.

DELISH
Mango Pie

🥣 Prep Time: 15 mins
🕑 Total Time: 2 hrs 20 mins

Servings per Recipe: 24
Calories   219 kcal
Fat   11.7 g
Carbohydrates   27.1g
Protein   2.5 g
Cholesterol   26 mg
Sodium   101 mg

Ingredients

2 C. all-purpose flour, sifted
1/2 C. confectioners' sugar
3/4 C. butter
1 (8 oz.) package cream cheese, softened
1/2 C. white sugar
1 tsp vanilla extract
3/4 (12 oz.) container whipped

topping
1 C. cold water
2 envelopes unflavored gelatin
1 C. boiling water
1/2 C. white sugar
1/4 tsp salt
1/4 C. lemon juice
5 C. diced mango

Directions

1. Set your oven to 350 degrees F before doing anything else.
2. In a bowl, mix together the flour and confectioners' sugar.
3. With a pastry cutter, cut the butter and mix till a coarse crumb forms.
4. Transfer the mixture into a 13x9-inch baking dish and cook everything in the oven for about 20-25 minutes. Remove everything from the oven and keep aside to cool completely.
5. In a bowl, add the cream cheese, 1/2 C. of the white sugar, and vanilla extract and beat till smooth. Fold in the whipped topping and place the mixture over the crust evenly.
6. Refrigerate for about 30 minutes.
7. In a bowl, add the cold water and sprinkle with the gelatin, then stir well.
8. Place the hot water over gelatin mixture and stir till the gelatin dissolves completely.
9. Add 1/2 C. of the sugar and salt into gelatin mixture and stir till the sugar dissolves.
10. Add the lemon juice and keep aside to cool.
11. Fold in the mango and refrigerate for about 15-20 minutes.
12. Pour mango gelatin over cream cheese filling and refrigerate for about 1 hour.

Comforting Mango Cobbler

🥣 Prep Time: 15 mins
🕐 Total Time: 1 hr

Servings per Recipe: 12
Calories   384 kcal
Fat   8.5 g
Carbohydrates   76.1g
Protein   3.4 g
Cholesterol   22 mg
Sodium   277 mg

Ingredients

Mangos:
8 mangoes - peeled, seeded, and sliced
2 C. water
1/2 C. white sugar
Batter:
2 C. white sugar
1/2 C. butter, softened

2 C. all-purpose flour
4 tsp baking powder
1/4 tsp salt
1 C. milk
1 tbsp vanilla extract

Directions

1. Set your oven to 375 degrees F before doing anything else.
2. In a pan, mix together the mangoes, 1/2 C. of the sugar and water on medium heat and simmer for about 5-6 minutes, stirring occasionally.
3. Drain the syrup from the mangoes, reserving in a bowl.
4. In a bowl, add the butter and 2 C. of the sugar and beat till creamy.
5. In another bowl mix together the flour, baking powder and salt.
6. Slowly, add the flour mixture and milk into the butter mixture and mix well.
7. Add the vanilla extract and mix till well combined.
8. Transfer the mixture into a 13x9-inch baking dish evenly and top with the mango slices.
9. Place bout 2 C. of the reserved syrup over the mangoes evenly and cook everything in the oven for about 40-45 minutes.

LUSCIOUS
Fruity Dessert

🥣 Prep Time: 10 mins
🕐 Total Time: 10 mins

Servings per Recipe: 8
Calories   192 kcal
Fat   11.4 g
Cholesterol   23.6g
Sodium   1.6 g
Carbohydrates   41 mg
Protein   13 mg

Ingredients

1 C. heavy whipping cream
1 tsp vanilla extract
2 ripe mangoes, peeled and chopped
3 bananas, thickly sliced
2 (6 oz.) containers fresh blueberries

Directions

1. In a bowl, add the cream and vanilla extract and beat till stiff peaks form.
2. The whipped cream will form sharp peaks by lifting the beater straight up.
3. Gently. Fold in the fruit.

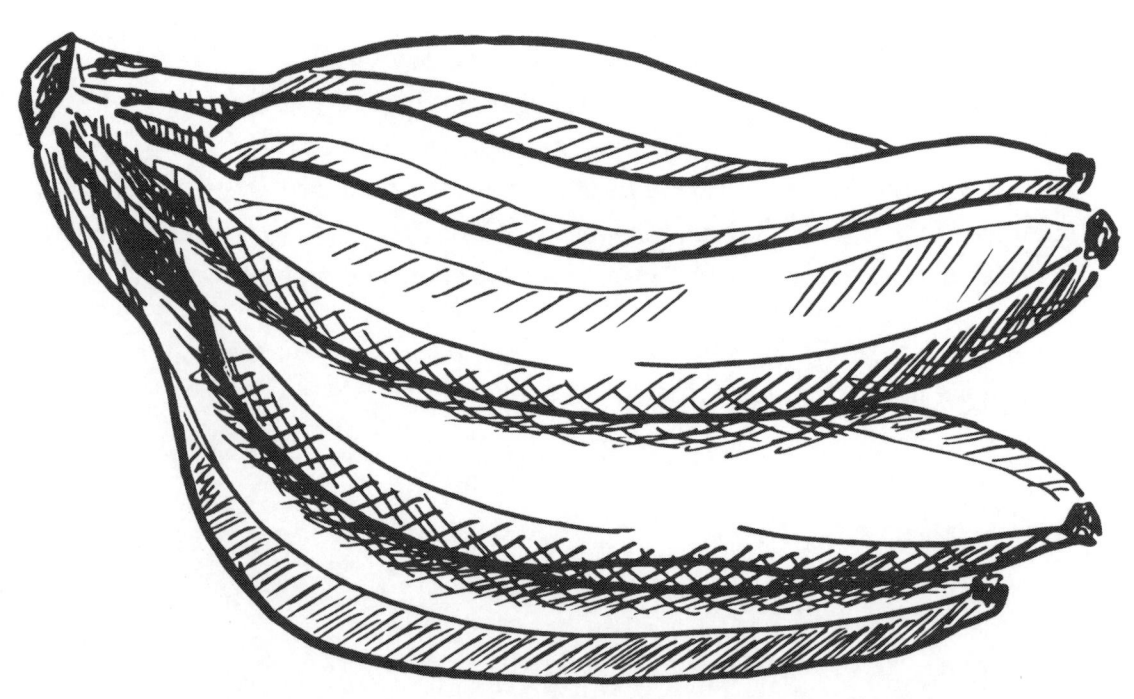

Delightful Summer Salsa

Prep Time: 20 mins
Total Time: 50 mins

Servings per Recipe: 4
Calories   112 kcal
Fat   7.5 g
Cholesterol   12.6g
Sodium   1.7 g
Carbohydrates 0 mg
Protein   9 mg

Ingredients

2 fresh peaches - peeled, pitted, and diced
1 jalapeno pepper, seeded and minced
1/2 red onion, minced
1/2 red bell pepper, minced
1/4 C. chopped fresh cilantro
2 cloves garlic, grated
1/2 lime, juiced
1/2 lemon, juiced
salt and ground black pepper to taste
1 avocado - peeled, pitted, and diced

Directions

1. In a large bowl, add all the ingredients except the avocado and gently stir to combine.
2. Refrigerate, covered for at least 30 minutes before serving.
3. Gently, fold in the avocado and serve.

REFRESHING
Fruity Sorbet

🥣 Prep Time: 10 mins
🕐 Total Time: 30 mins

Servings per Recipe: 6
Calories 63 kcal
Fat 0 g
Cholesterol 16.3g
Sodium 0.1 g
Carbohydrates 0 mg
Protein 1 mg

Ingredients

3 peaches, peeled and diced
1 1/2 tbsp orange juice
1/2 C. diced pineapple

1/2 C. simple syrup

Directions

1. In a food processor add the orange juice and peaches and pulse till smooth.
2. Add the pineapple and syrup pulse till a smooth puree forms.
3. Transfer the mixture into an ice cream maker and freeze according to manufacturer's directions.

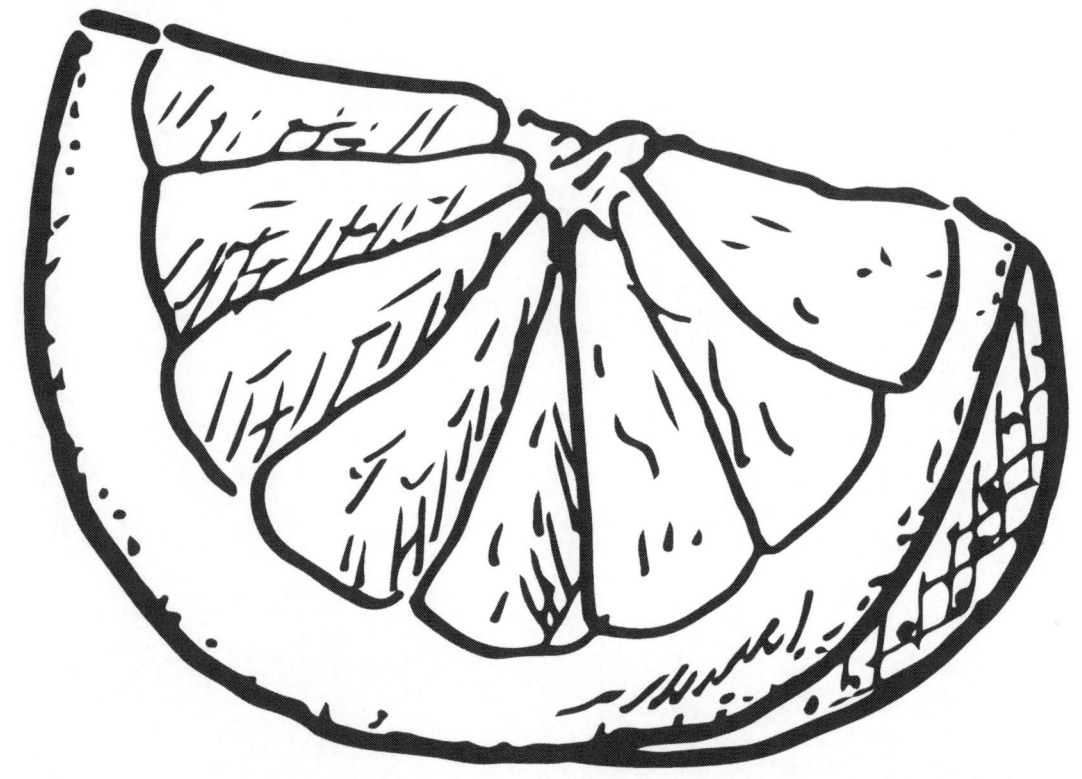

Special Peach Treat

Prep Time: 10 mins
Total Time: 15 mins

Servings per Recipe: 2
Calories	477 kcal
Fat	31.3 g
Carbohydrates	31.2g
Protein	18.2 g
Cholesterol	45 mg
Sodium	812 mg

Ingredients

2 (1 inch thick) slices French bread, toasted
2 tbsp olive oil, divided, or as needed
4 oz. fresh goat cheese, softened
2 tsp fresh thyme leaves, or to taste
salt and freshly ground black pepper to taste
6 fresh peach slices

Directions

1. Set your oven to the broiler and arrange oven rack about 6-inches from the heating element.
2. Line a baking sheet with the foil.
3. Drizzle the bread slices with 1 tsp of the oil from both the sides and place onto the prepared baking sheet.
4. In a bowl, mix together the goat cheese, thyme and black pepper.
5. Spread the cheese mixture over both the slices evenly and top with the peach slices evenly.
6. Drizzle with the remaining oil and cook under the broiler for about 2 minutes.

ITALIAN Peach Bruschetta

🥣 Prep Time: 10 mins
🕒 Total Time: 15 mins

Servings per Recipe: 12
Calories   105 kcal
Fat   3.7 g
Carbohydrates   12.7 g
Protein   3.8 g
Cholesterol   10 mg
Sodium   300 mg

Ingredients

1 tsp herbes de Provence
1 tsp sea salt
12 slices Italian bread, toasted
6 oz. Burrata cheese
1 large fresh freestone peach, cut into 12 slices
2 tbsp turbinado sugar

Directions

1. In a small bowl, mix together the herbes de Provence and salt and keep aside.
2. Spread the Burrata cheese over each toasted bread slice and sprinkle a pinch of the herbes de Provence mixture.
3. In a heat proof plate, arrange the peach slices in a single layer.
4. Lightly sprinkle each peach slice with the turbinado sugar.
5. Set a kitchen torch to a medium-low flame and melt the sugar by making short, even passes over the top of the sugar.
6. Continue melting for about 30 seconds.
7. Place peach slice on each piece of toast and serve.

Refreshing Peach Salad

🥣 Prep Time: 10 mins
🕐 Total Time: 10 mins

Servings per Recipe: 6
Calories   191 kcal
Fat   17.3 g
Cholesterol   4.2g
Sodium   6.1 g
Carbohydrates   15 mg
Protein   176 mg

Ingredients

2 tbsp olive oil
1 tbsp rice vinegar
1 tbsp apple cider vinegar
1 tsp mayonnaise
salt and ground black pepper to taste
1 small head escarole, cut into 1-inch ribbons
1 peach, sliced
4 oz. goat cheese, crumbled
1/2 C. toasted walnuts

Directions

1. In a bowl, add oil, mayonnaise, both vinegars, salt and black pepper and beat till well combined.
2. In a large serving bowl, add the remaining ingredients.
3. Add the vinaigrette and toss to coat well.

GOURMET
Fall-Time Dessert

🥣 Prep Time: 30 mins
🕒 Total Time: 1 hr 45 mins

Servings per Recipe: 8
Calories   317 kcal
Fat   10.8 g
Carbohydrates   50.9 g
Protein   2.6 g
Cholesterol   15 mg
Sodium   151 mg

Ingredients

6 sweet potatoes, peeled and sliced 1/2 inch thick
1 (16 oz.) package frozen unsweetened peach slices, thawed
4 tbsp butter, sliced into pats
1 tbsp lemon juice
1/2 C. brown sugar
1/2 tsp ground ginger
salt
1/4 C. coffee flavored liqueur
1/2 C. chopped pecans

Directions

1. Set your oven to 350 degrees F before doing anything else and lightly, grease a 13x9-inch baking dish.
2. In the bottom of the prepared baking dish, place half of the sweet potato slices, followed by the half of the peach slices.
3. Place half of the butter over peach slices in the form of dots.
4. Repeat the layers of the sweet potato and peach slices and drizzle with the lemon juice.
5. In a bowl, mix together the brown sugar, ginger and salt.
6. Spread the brown sugar mixture over the peach slices evenly.
7. Place the remaining butter on top in the form of dots and drizzle with the liqueur.
8. With foil, cover the baking dish and cook in the oven for about 1 hour.
9. Uncover the baking dish and top with the pecans.
10. Cook in the oven for about 10-15 minutes.

Tasty Chicken Polynesian Style

🥣 Prep Time: 20 mins
🕐 Total Time: 1 hr 25 mins

Servings per Recipe: 6
Calories   478 kcal
Fat   26.7 g
Carbohydrates   25.8 g
Protein   33.8 g
Cholesterol   97 mg
Sodium   449 mg

Ingredients

1/2 C. all-purpose flour
1/2 tsp salt
1/4 tsp ground black pepper
3 lb. bone-in chicken pieces
1/4 C. corn oil
1 1/2 C. water
1 onion, chopped
1 green bell pepper, cut into strips

1 (15 oz.) can peach halves, liquid reserved
1 tbsp soy sauce
3 tbsp distilled white vinegar
1 tbsp cornstarch
4 tomatoes, chopped
salt and black pepper to taste

Directions

1. In a seal able bag, mix together the flour, salt and black pepper.
2. Add the chicken and seal the bag, then shake to coat well.
3. Remove the chicken
4. In a Dutch oven, heat the corn oil on medium heat

ASIAN STYLE
Peach Soup

🍲 Prep Time: 25 mins
🕐 Total Time: 1 hr 30 mins

Servings per Recipe: 4
Calories   523 kcal
Fat   40.4 g
Carbohydrates   26.3g
Protein   17.5 g
Cholesterol   206 mg
Sodium   437 mg

Ingredients

5 tbsp olive oil
2 tbsp Madras curry powder
1 large onion, minced
3 cloves garlic, minced
1 (15 oz.) can sliced peaches in syrup, chopped
1 (14.5 oz.) can chopped plum tomatoes
1 tsp ground ginger
1 C. cream
1 C. vegetable broth
salt and black pepper to taste
2 C. lettuce, chopped
2 C. shelled, cooked shrimp

Directions

1. In a large pan, heat the oil on medium heat.
2. Add the curry powder and sauté for about 1 minute.
3. Add the onion and sauté for about 8-10 minutes.
4. Stir in the peaches with the syrup, cream, tomatoes, ginger, broth, salt and black pepper and reduce the heat to low.
5. Simmer for about 45 minutes.
6. Serve hot with a topping of the shrimp and lettuce.

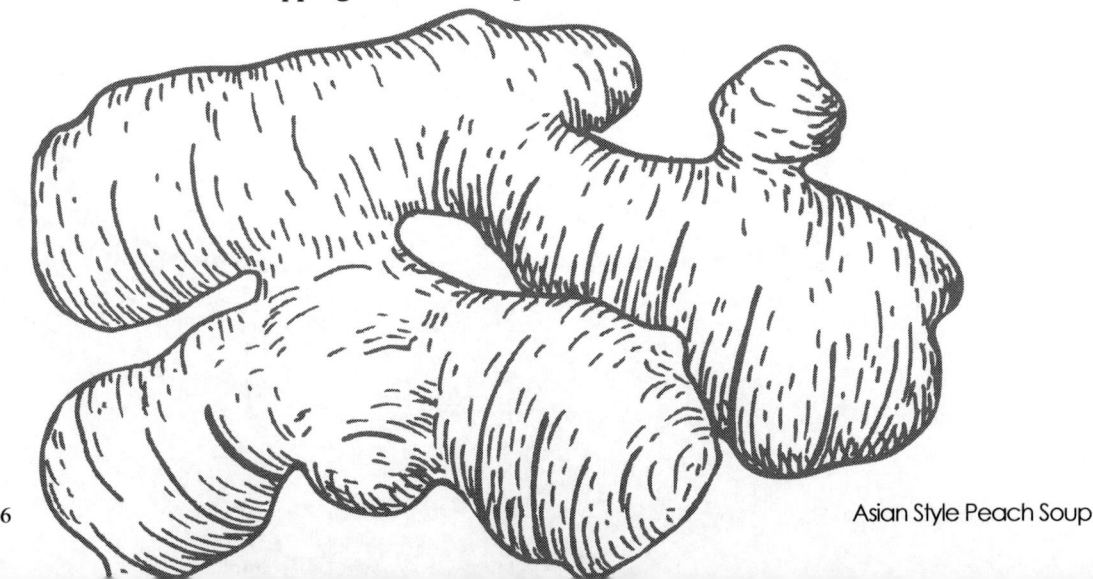

Deliciously Glazed Chicken

 Prep Time: 15 mins
 Total Time: 40 mins

Servings per Recipe: 4
Calories	266 kcal
Fat	7.2 g
Carbohydrates	21.1g
Protein	27.2 g
Cholesterol	72 mg
Sodium	274 mg

Ingredients

- 1 (15 oz.) can sliced peaches
- 4 skinless, boneless chicken breast halves
- 1 tbsp olive oil
- 1/2 C. red bell pepper, diced
- 1/2 C. chunky salsa
- 1 tbsp frozen orange juice concentrate, thawed
- salt and pepper to taste

Directions

1. Drain the peach slices, reserving the syrup.
2. Sprinkle the chicken with the salt and black pepper evenly.
3. In a large skillet, heat the oil on medium heat and cook the chicken for about 9-10 minutes, flipping once in the middle way.
4. Transfer the chicken into a bowl.
5. In the same skillet, add the bell pepper on medium-low heat and sauté for about 2 minutes.
6. Stir in the salsa, orange juice and reserved peach syrup and bring to a boil, scraping the brown bits.
7. Stir in the peaches and cook till heated completely.
8. Stir in the cooked chicken and cot with the glaze evenly.
9. Serve immediately.

CHUNKY Fruit Chutney

🍲 Prep Time: 35 mins
🕐 Total Time: 2 hrs 35 mins

Servings per Recipe:	64
Calories	18 kcal
Fat	0.1 g
Carbohydrates	4.3g
Protein	0.4 g
Cholesterol	0 mg
Sodium	113 mg

Ingredients

15 tomatoes, peeled and chopped
5 fresh peaches - peeled, pitted and chopped
5 red apples - peeled, cored and diced
4 medium onions, diced
4 stalks celery, diced
1 1/2 C. distilled white vinegar
1 tbsp salt
1 C. pickling spice, wrapped in cheesecloth

Directions

1. In a large pan, mix together all the ingredients and bring to a boil.
2. Reduce the heat to low and simmer for about 2 hours.
3. Transfer the mixture into the sterile jars and refrigerate store.

Lancaster Strawberries

Prep Time: 5 mins
Total Time: 5 mins

Servings per Recipe: 4
Calories   401.0
Fat   41.4g
Cholesterol   144.0mg
Sodium   204.9mg
Carbohydrates   4.0g
Protein   4.5g

Ingredients

- 8 oz. cream cheese
- 1 C. whipping cream
- 1/2 tsp vanilla extract
- Strawberry, 1 C. for each serving
- Powdered sugar
- Mint leaves

Directions

1. In a bowl, add the cream cheese and beat till softened.
2. Slowly, add the cream and beat till the mixture is smooth.
3. Stir in the vanilla extract and powdered sugar.
4. Wash and hull the strawberries and transfer into another bowl.
5. Refrigerate the bowls of strawberries and cream mixture till serving.
6. Divide the strawberries into serving dishes bowls and top with the cream mixture.
7. Serve with a garnishing of the garnish mint leaves.

GREATLY-FLAVORED
Muffins

🥣 Prep Time: 25 mins
🕐 Total Time: 50 mins

Servings per Recipe: 16
Calories   351 kcal
Fat   18.2 g
Carbohydrates   44.3g
Protein   3.6 g
Cholesterol   35 mg
Sodium   238 mg

Ingredients

3 C. all-purpose flour
1 tbsp ground cinnamon
1 tsp baking soda
1 tsp salt
1 1/4 C. vegetable oil
3 eggs, lightly beaten

2 C. white sugar
2 C. peeled, pitted, and chopped peaches

Directions

1. Set your oven to 400 degrees F before doing anything else and grease 16 cups of the muffin tins.
2. In a large bowl, mix together the flour, baking soda, cinnamon and salt.
3. In another bowl, add the sugar, eggs and oil and beat till well combined.
4. Add the egg mixture into the flour mixture and mix till well combined.
5. Gently, fold in the peaches and transfer the mixture into the prepared muffin cups.
6. Cook in the oven for about 25 minutes.

Fantastic Peach Bread

Prep Time: 30 mins
Total Time: 1 hr 30 mins

Servings per Recipe: 20
Calories   203 kcal
Fat   10.1 g
Carbohydrates   26.6 g
Protein   2.6 g
Cholesterol   31 mg
Sodium   157 mg

Ingredients

1 1/2 C. white sugar
1/2 C. butter
2 eggs
2 1/2 C. pureed peaches
2 C. all-purpose flour
1 tsp baking soda
1 tsp baking powder
1/2 tsp ground cinnamon
1/4 tsp salt
1 tsp almond extract
1 1/4 C. chopped toasted pecans

Directions

1. Set your oven to 325 degrees F before doing anything else and grease a 9x5-inch loaf pan.
2. In a large bowl, add the butter and sugar and beat till creamy.
3. Add the eggs, one at a time and beat till fluffy and light.
4. Stir in the peach puree.
5. Add the remaining ingredients except the pecans and mix till well combined.
6. Gently, fold in the pecans and transfer the mixture into the prepared loaf pan.
7. Cook in the oven for about 50-60 minutes.
8. Remove from the oven and keep on the wire rack for about 10 minutes before removing from the loaf pan.

GERMAN
Peach Pancakes

🥣 Prep Time: 15 mins
🕐 Total Time: 44 mins

Servings per Recipe: 6
Calories   273 kcal
Fat   9 g
Carbohydrates   42.5g
Protein   5.8 g
Cholesterol   110 mg
Sodium   287 mg

Ingredients

1 (15.25 oz.) can Del Monte(R) Sliced Peaches in Heavy Syrup
3 eggs
1/3 C. sugar
2 tbsp butter, melted
1 tsp finely shredded lemon zest
1/2 tsp salt
2/3 C. all-purpose flour
2/3 C. milk

1 tbsp butter
1 1/2 C. fresh blueberries
Powdered sugar
1 tbsp finely shredded fresh basil

Directions

1. Set your oven to 325 degrees F before doing anything else.
2. Drain the peaches, reserving about 1/4 C. of the syrup.
3. In a bowl, add the sugar, eggs, 2 tbsp of the melted butter, lemon zest and salt and beat till well combined.
4. Add the milk and flour and beat till well combined.
5. In a 10-inch oven proof skillet, melt 1 tbsp of the butter on medium heat.
6. Add the flour mixture and immediately, place the peach slices over the mixture evenly then transfer the skillet into the oven.
7. Cook in the oven for about 25-30 minutes.
8. Meanwhile for compote in a pan, add the blueberries and reserved peach syrup on medium heat and cook for about 4-5 minutes.
9. While serving, sprinkle the pancakes with the powdered sugar and basil and serve alongside the blueberry compote.

Overnight Peach French Toast Casserole

Prep Time: 9 hrs
Total Time: 9 hrs 45 mins

Servings per Recipe: 8
Calories   362 kcal
Fat   15 g
Carbohydrates   51.3 g
Protein   7.2 g
Cholesterol   147 mg
Sodium   276 mg

Ingredients

- 1 C. packed brown sugar
- 1/2 C. butter
- 2 tbsp water
- 1 (29 oz.) can sliced peaches, drained
- 12 (3/4 inch thick) slices day-old French bread
- 5 eggs
- 1 tbsp vanilla extract
- 1 pinch ground cinnamon

Directions

1. In a pan, mix together the butter, brown sugar and water and bring to a boil.
2. Reduce the heat to low and simmer, stirring occasionally for about 10 minutes.
3. Transfer the brown sugar mixture in the bottom of a 13x9-inch baking dish evenly.
4. Arrange the peach slices over the sugar coating in a layer and top with the bread slices.
5. In a medium bowl, add the eggs and vanilla and beat well.
6. Place the egg mixture over the bread slices evenly and top with the cinnamon.
7. Refrigerate, covered for about 8 hours or overnight.
8. Remove the dish from the refrigerator and keep aside in the room temperature for about 30 minutes.
9. Set your oven to 425 degrees F.
10. Cook in the oven for about 25-30 minutes.

FRENCH STYLE
Candy

🥣 Prep Time: 10 mins
🕐 Total Time: 8 hrs 30 mins

Servings per Recipe: 25
Calories   81 kcal
Fat   0 g
Carbohydrates   21g
Protein   0 g
Cholesterol   0 mg
Sodium   1 mg

Ingredients

1 lb. ripe peaches - peeled, pitted and sliced
1 tbsp lime juice
2 C. white sugar, divided

3 tbsp liquid pectin
1/2 C. white sugar, for sprinkling

Directions

1. Line an 8x8-inch baking dish with the plastic wrap.
2. In a blender, add peaches and lemon juice and pulse till smooth.
3. Transfer the peach mixture in a pan on medium heat.
4. Stir in the 1/2 C. of the sugar and bring to a boil.
5. Stir in the pectin and remaining 1/2 C. of the sugar and heat to 205 degrees F.
6. Cook for about 10 minutes, stirring continuously.
7. Remove from the heat and transfer the mixture into the prepared baking dish.
8. Shake the baking dish gently and then, tap on the counter top to remove the air bubbles.
9. Refrigerate, covered for about 8 hours.
10. Spread about 1/4 C. of the sugar over a silicon baking mat evenly.
11. Carefully, invert the peach mix over the sugar.
12. Remove the plastic wrap and spread the remaining sugar on top.
13. Cut the mix into equal sized 25 squares.

Satisfying Peach Crumble

Prep Time: 35 mins
Total Time: 1 hr 25 mins

Servings per Recipe: 8
Calories   319 kcal
Fat   23.3 g
Carbohydrates   26.2g
Protein   4.5 g
Cholesterol   15 mg
Sodium   231 mg

Ingredients

2 tsp coconut oil, melted
8 fresh peaches
1/4 C. coconut sugar
2 tsp arrowroot powder
1 tsp ground cinnamon
1/2 tsp ground allspice
Crumble Topping:
1 C. almond flour
1/2 C. chopped pecans
1/2 C. unsweetened shredded coconut

1/4 C. coconut sugar
1 tsp sea salt
1 tsp ground cinnamon
1/4 C. unsalted butter, chilled and cut into small cubes

Directions

1. Set your oven to 350 degrees F before doing anything else and lightly, grease a 13x9-inch baking dish.
2. Cut the each peach in half, keeping pit intact.
3. In a large pan, add the water and bring to a boil.
4. Remove from the heat and immediately, add the peaches for about 10 minutes.
5. Remove from the pan and keep aside to cool.
6. In a small bowl, mix together the arrowroot powder, 1/4 C. of the coconut sugar, cinnamon and allspice.
7. In another large bowl, mix together the almond flour, coconut, pecans, remaining coconut sugar, cinnamon and salt.
8. With your fingers, rub the cold butter till the mixture becomes crumbly.
9. Remove pit from the peach halves and peel them, then cut the flesh in the slices.
10. Place the peach slices into the prepared baking dish and sprinkle with the coconut sugar mixture. Spread the flour mixture on top evenly.
11. Cook in the oven for about 35-40 minutes.

DELICIOUS Fruity Tartlets

🥣 Prep Time: 10 mins
🕐 Total Time: 32 mins

Servings per Recipe: 18
Calories   185 kcal
Fat   10.4 g
Carbohydrates   21.5g
Protein   2.1 g
Cholesterol   0 mg
Sodium   74 mg

Ingredients

1 (17.3 oz.) package frozen puff pastry, thawed
2 peaches - peeled, pitted, and thinly sliced
3/4 C. apricot preserves, divided
2 tsp hot water

Directions

1. Set your oven to 425 degrees F before doing anything else and line 2 baking sheets with the parchment papers.
2. Cut each sheet of the puff pastry into 9 (3-inch) squares.
3. Place about a small amount of the apricot preserves in the middle of each square.
4. Arrange 3 slices of peach over the preserves in a fan shape, leaving a little border of pastry exposed.
5. Place a small amount of apricot preserves over the peach slices.
6. Cook in the oven, 1 baking sheet at a time for about 10 minutes.
7. For glaze in a small bowl, mix together the remaining apricot preserves and hot water.
8. Place some of the glaze over each baked tartlet and cook in the oven for about 2 minute further.
9. Repeat with the second baking sheet.

Homemade Asian Plum Sauce

🍜 Prep Time: 5 mins
🕐 Total Time: 20 mins

Servings per Recipe: 10
Calories   102 kcal
Fat   0.1 g
Carbohydrates   25.1 g
Protein   0.2 g
Cholesterol   0 mg
Sodium   11 mg

Ingredients

3/4 (16 oz.) jar plum jam
2 tbsp vinegar
1 tbsp brown sugar
1 tbsp dried minced onion
1 tsp crushed red pepper flakes

1 clove garlic, minced
1/2 tsp ground ginger

Directions

1. In a pan, mix together the jam, vinegar, brown sugar, dried onion, red pepper, garlic and ginger on medium heat and bring to a boil, stirring continuously.
2. Remove from the heat.

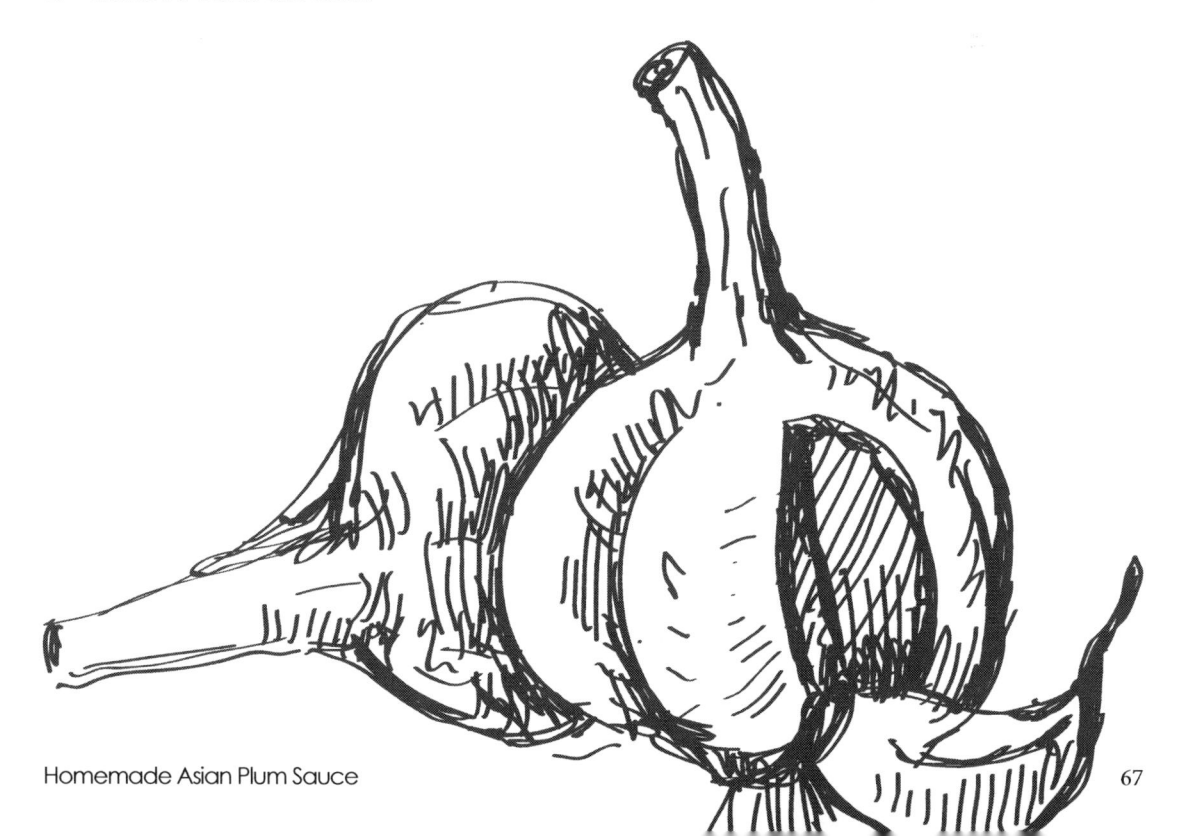

COUNTRYSIDE
Plum Crisp

🥣 Prep Time: 15 mins
🕐 Total Time: 55 mins

Servings per Recipe: 6
Calories 414 kcal
Fat 16.7 g
Carbohydrates 64.7g
Protein 4.3 g
Cholesterol 72 mg
Sodium 631 mg

Ingredients

12 plums, pitted and chopped
1 C. white sugar, divided
1 C. sifted all-purpose flour
1 1/2 tsp baking powder
1 tsp salt
1 beaten egg
1/2 C. melted butter

Directions

1. Set your oven to 350 degrees F before doing anything else and grease an 8x8-inch baking dish.
2. In the bottom of the prepared baking dish, arrange the chopped plums and sprinkle with 1/4 C. of the sugar.
3. In a bowl, mix together 3/4 C. of the white sugar, flour, baking powder and salt.
4. Add the beaten egg and mix till combined.
5. Place the flour mixture over the plums evenly and drizzle with the melted butter.
6. Cook in the oven for about 40 minutes.

Potato and Plum Dumplings

🥣 Prep Time: 1 hr 30 mins
🕒 Total Time: 2 hrs 15 mins

Servings per Recipe: 16
Calories   231 kcal
Fat   4 g
Carbohydrates   44.6 g
Protein   5.3 g
Cholesterol   19 mg
Sodium   80 mg

Ingredients

- 3 tbsp butter
- 1 C. dry bread crumbs
- 4 large russet potatoes, peeled
- 1 tbsp butter
- 2 C. all-purpose flour
- 1 egg
- 1 pinch salt
- 16 Italian prune plums, pitted and left whole
- 16 tsp white sugar, divided

Directions

1. In a skillet, melt 3 tbsp of the butter on medium-low heat and stir fry the bread crumbs for about 2 minutes. Remove from the heat and keep aside.
2. In a pan of water, add the potatoes on medium heat and boil for about 20-30 minutes.
3. Drain the potatoes and keep aside to cool for several minutes.
4. Through a potato ricer, squeeze the potatoes into a bowl.
5. Add 1 tbsp of the butter into the potatoes and let it melt.
6. Add the flour and mix till well combined. Add the egg and salt and mix well.
7. Place the potato mixture onto a generously floured surface and knead for about 10 minutes.
8. Divide the dough into quarters and subdivide each quarter into fourths to make 16 portions.
9. Make a ball from each portion and roll the ball out on a floured surface to form a 3 1/2-inches circle.
10. Place a pitted plum in the center of each circle and place a tsp of sugar into each plum.
11. Roll and pinch the dough around the plum to seal.
12. In a pan, add the lightly salted water and bring to a boil on medium heat.
13. Add the dumplings into the boiling water and boil for about 5 minutes.
14. With a slotted spoon, gently remove the dumplings and roll in the toasted bread crumbs.

EASY Homemade Plum Cake

🥣 Prep Time: 30 mins
🕐 Total Time: 1 hr 15 mins

Servings per Recipe: 12
Calories   522 kcal
Fat   20.1 g
Carbohydrates   80.9 g
Protein   6.8 g
Cholesterol   82 mg
Sodium   337 mg

Ingredients

7 C. pitted and quartered plums
2/3 C. butter, softened
1 1/2 C. white sugar
2 eggs
3 C. sifted all-purpose flour
1 tbsp baking powder
1/2 tsp salt
2 C. milk
2 tsp vanilla extract

1 C. white sugar
1/2 C. butter, softened
1/4 C. all-purpose flour
1 tsp cinnamon

Directions

1. Set your oven to 350 degrees F before doing anything else and grease a 13x9-inch baking dish.
2. Arrange the plums into the bottom of the prepared baking dish.
3. In a large bowl, add 2/3 C. of the butter, 1 1/2 C. of the white sugar and mix till a smooth and creamy mixture forms.
4. Add the eggs, one at a time, beating continuously.
5. Stir in 3 C. of the flour, baking powder and salt.
6. Add the milk and vanilla extract and mix till a smooth mixture forms.
7. Place the mixture over the plums evenly.
8. In a bowl, add 1 C. of the sugar, 1/2 C. of the butter, 1/4 C. of the flour and cinnamon and mix till a crumbly topping forms.
9. Spread the topping over the mixture.
10. Cook in the oven for about 45-50 minutes or till a toothpick inserted in the center comes out clean.

Cinnamon Clove and Plum Bread

🥣 Prep Time: 10 mins
🕐 Total Time: 1 hr 30 mins

Servings per Recipe: 12
Calories   510 kcal
Fat   26.2 g
Carbohydrates   66.7 g
Protein   5.3 g
Cholesterol   46 mg
Sodium   170 mg

Ingredients

- 1 C. vegetable oil
- 3 eggs
- 2 (6 oz.) jars plum baby food
- 2 C. white sugar
- 1 tsp red food coloring
- 2 C. all-purpose flour
- 1 tsp ground cloves
- 1 tsp ground cinnamon
- 1/2 tsp ground allspice
- 1/2 tsp salt
- 1/2 tsp baking soda
- 1 C. chopped walnuts
- 1 C. confectioners' sugar
- 2 1/2 tbsp lemon juice

Directions

1. Set your oven to 350 degrees F before doing anything else and grease and flour bundt pan.
2. In a large bowl, mix together the vegetable oil, white sugar, eggs, baby food and food coloring.
3. In another bowl, mix together flour, cloves, cinnamon, allspice, salt, baking soda and nuts.
4. Add the egg mixture into the flour mixture and mix till well combined.
5. Transfer the mixture into the prepared bundt pan.
6. Cook in the oven for about 50-60 minutes or till a toothpick inserted in the center comes out clean.
7. Remove from the oven and cool for about 10 minutes before turning out onto wire rack to cool.
8. In a bowl, mix together the confectioner's sugar and lemon juice.
9. Brush the top of hot cake with the lemon mixture.

GERMAN Plum Cake (Kuchen)

🥣 Prep Time: 15 mins
🕐 Total Time: 50 mins

Servings per Recipe: 12
Calories   232 kcal
Fat   5.6 g
Carbohydrates   43.5g
Protein   3.1 g
Cholesterol   31 mg
Sodium   153 mg

Ingredients

Batter:
1/2 C. white sugar
2 tbsp margarine
2 eggs, beaten
1 C. all-purpose flour
1 tsp baking powder
1/4 tsp salt
1 tsp vanilla extract
10 Italian plums, halved and pitted

Topping:
1 C. white sugar
1/2 C. all-purpose flour
3 tbsp margarine, melted
1/2 tsp ground cinnamon

Directions

1. Set your oven to 375 degrees F before doing anything else and grease and flour an 11x7-inch baking dish.
2. In a bowl, add 1/2 C. of the sugar and 2 tbsp of the margarine and with an electric mixer, beat till smooth and creamy.
3. Add the eggs, 1 C. of the flour, baking powder and salt and vanilla and mix till well combined.
4. Transfer the mixture into the prepared baking dish and top with the plums, skin side-down.
5. In a bowl, add 1 C. of the sugar, 1/2 C. of the flour, 3 tbsp of the margarine and cinnamon and mix till a crumbly mixture forms.
6. Place the crumbly mixture over the plums.
7. Cook in the oven for about 35 minutes.

A Very Light Flan

Prep Time: 15 mins
Total Time: 3 hrs 50 mins

Servings per Recipe: 5
Calories   148 kcal
Fat   2.1 g
Carbohydrates   30.6 g
Protein   3.4 g
Cholesterol   7 mg
Sodium   30 mg

Ingredients

2 C. plums, pitted and sliced
1 tbsp water (optional)
1 (.25 oz.) package unflavored pectin
1/2 C. hot water
1/2 C. white sugar
2 tbsp lemon juice
1/2 C. evaporated milk

Directions

1. In a pan, add the plums on medium-low heat and simmer, covered for about 5-10 minutes, stirring occasionally.
2. If the mixture becomes too thick or starts to burn, add a tbsp of water.
3. Remove from the heat and keep aside to cool.
4. In a bowl, add the pectin and 1/2 C. of the hot water and stir to dissolve.
5. Add the cooled plums, sugar and lemon juice and mix till the pectin and sugar are dissolved.
6. Refrigerate to chill for about 30 minutes.
7. In a bowl, add the evaporated milk and with an electric mixer, beat till thick.
8. Gently, add the whipped milk into the plum mixture and with electric mixer beat till fluffy and well combined.
9. Refrigerate to chill for at least 3 hours before serving.

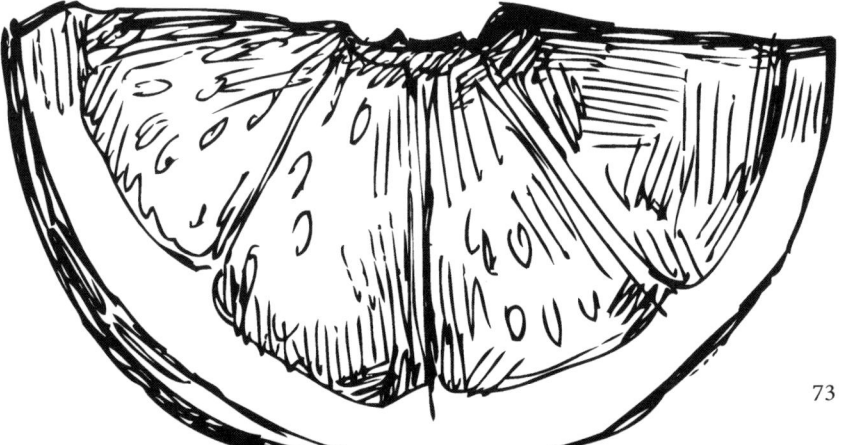

PLUM JELLY 101

🥣 Prep Time: 30 mins
🕐 Total Time: 2 hrs 50 mins

Servings per Recipe: 128
Calories   48 kcal
Fat   0 g
Carbohydrates   12.4g
Protein   0 g
Cholesterol   1 mg
Sodium   1 mg

Ingredients

4 1/2 C. pitted, chopped plums
1/2 C. water
7 1/2 C. white sugar
1/2 tsp butter (optional)
1 (1.75 oz.) package powdered fruit pectin
8 half-pint canning jars with lids and rings

Directions

1. In a large pan, add the plums and water and bring to a boil.
2. Reduce the heat to medium-low and simmer, covered for about 5 minutes.
3. Stir in the sugar, then add the butter to reduce the foaming.
4. Bring them to a full, rolling boil over high heat, stirring continuously.
5. Immediately, stir in the pectin and bring to a full boil.
6. Boil for about 1 minute, stirring continuously.
7. Remove from the heat and skim off and discard any foam.
8. Sterilize the jars and lids in boiling water for at least 5 minutes.
9. Place the plum jam into the hot, sterilized jars, filling the jars to within 1/8-inch of the top.
10. Run a knife around the insides of the jars to remove any air bubbles.
11. With a moist paper towel, wipe the rims of the jars to remove any food residue.
12. Top with lids and screw on rings.
13. Place a rack in the bottom of a large pan and fill halfway with the water and bring to a boil on high heat.
14. With a holder carefully, lower the jars into the pan, leave a 2-inch space between the jars.
15. Bring the water to a full boil and process, covered for about 10 minutes.
16. Remove the jars from the pan and place onto a wood surface, several inches apart to cool.
17. After cooling, press the top of each lid with a finger, ensuring that the seal is tight.
18. Store in a cool, dark area. Refrigerate opened jars for up to 3 weeks.

How to Make Tapioca Pudding

- Prep Time: 15 mins
- Total Time: 50 mins

Servings per Recipe: 6
Calories	468 kcal
Fat	13 g
Carbohydrates	86.1g
Protein	5.1 g
Cholesterol	2 mg
Sodium	641 mg

Ingredients

- 12 plums, pitted and halved
- 1 C. white sugar
- 1/2 C. water
- 2 tbsp tapioca
- 1/2 tsp ground cinnamon
- 2 1/4 C. all-purpose baking mix
- 3 tbsp white sugar
- 2/3 C. milk
- 3 tbsp margarine, melted

Directions

1. Set your oven to 350 degrees F before doing anything else.
2. In a 2 quart baking dish, mix together the plums, 1 C. of the sugar, water, tapioca and cinnamon.
3. Cook in the oven for about 25 minutes.
4. Now, set the oven temperature to 450 degrees F.
5. In a bowl, add the baking mix, 3 tbsp of the sugar, milk and melted margarine and mix till a biscuit dough forms.
6. With spoonfuls, place the mixture over the plum mixture.
7. Cook in the oven for about 10 minutes.
8. Remove from the oven and keep aside to cool slightly before serving.

RUSTIC Pie

🥣 Prep Time: 30 mins
🕐 Total Time: 1 hr 30 mins

Servings per Recipe: 8
Calories	685 kcal
Fat	24.9 g
Carbohydrates	109.1g
Protein	9.5 g
Cholesterol	99 mg
Sodium	424 mg

Ingredients

- 3 C. all-purpose flour
- 3/4 C. white sugar
- 2 1/2 tsp baking powder
- 1/8 tsp salt
- 2/3 C. butter
- 2 eggs
- 1 tsp vanilla extract
- 3 tbsp milk
- 1/2 tsp lemon zest
- 1/2 C. all-purpose flour
- 1/4 C. packed brown sugar
- 1/2 tsp ground cinnamon
- 1/4 tsp salt

- 1/3 C. chopped hazelnuts
- 1 tsp lemon zest
- 3 tbsp butter
- 5 C. plums, pitted and sliced
- 1 C. white sugar
- 1/4 C. all-purpose flour
- 1 tsp ground cinnamon
- 1/2 tsp ground allspice

Directions

1. Set your oven to 375 degrees F before doing anything else.
2. For crust in a large bowl, mix together 3 C. of the flour, 3/4 C. of the white sugar, baking powder and 1/8 tsp of the salt.
3. With a pastry cutter, cut in 2/3 C. butter till pieces are the size of small peas.
4. Add the eggs, vanilla extract, milk and lemon zest and mix till just combined.
5. Refrigerate the dough till serving.
6. For streusel topping in a bowl mix together 1/2 C. of the flour, brown sugar, 1/2 tsp of the cinnamon, 1/4 tsp of the salt, chopped nuts and grated lemon zest.
7. Add the butter and with the fingers, mix till all the Ingredients are well combined.
8. For fruit filling in a large bowl, add the pitted and sliced fruit.
9. In a small bowl, mix together the remaining sugar, flour, cinnamon, and allspice.
10. Place the sugar mixture over the fruit and stir gently until all fruit is evenly coated.
11. Roll out pie crust and arrange in a 9-inch pie pan.

12. Trim and flute the edges.
13. Place the fruit filling over the crust and top with the streusel topping evenly.
14. Cook in the oven for about 45-55 minutes.
15. Serve warm or at room temperature.

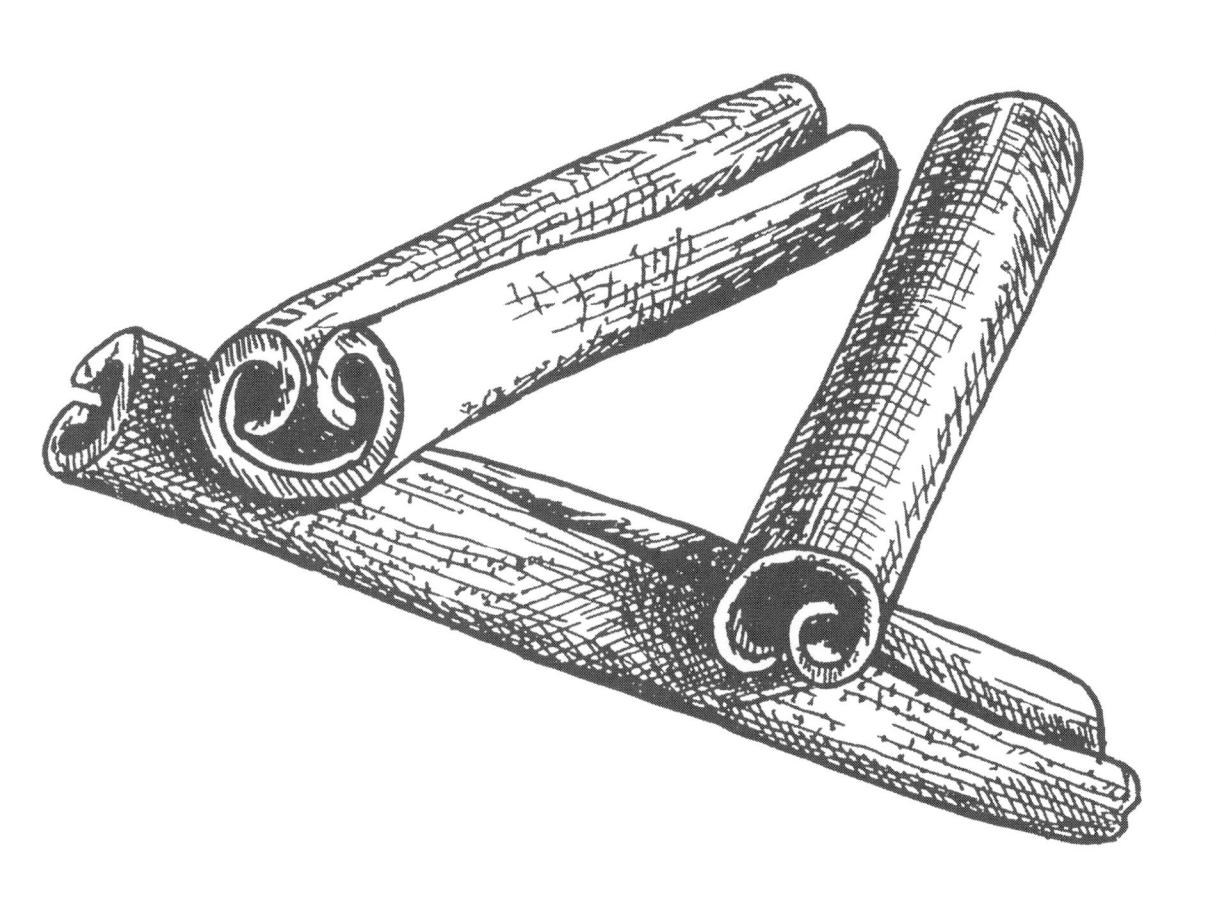

MOIST Homemade Plum Lemon Cake

🥣 Prep Time: 10 mins
🕒 Total Time: 1 hr 10 mins

Servings per Recipe: 12
Calories   164 kcal
Fat   9.1 g
Carbohydrates   18.4g
Protein   2.9 g
Cholesterol   67 mg
Sodium   93 mg

Ingredients

- 3 eggs, whites and yolks separated
- 1/2 C. butter, softened
- 1/2 C. white sugar
- 1 tsp lemon zest
- 1 C. all-purpose flour
- 1/2 tsp baking powder
- 1 1/4 C. plums, pitted and sliced

Directions

1. Set your oven to 375 degrees F before doing anything else and grease and flour a 9-inch tube pan.
2. In a small bowl, add the egg whites and beat till stiff peaks form.
3. In a large bowl, add the butter and sugar and beat till creamy and smooth.
4. Add the egg yolks and lemon zest and beat to combine.
5. In another bowl, mix together the flour and baking powder.
6. Add the flour mixture into the butter mixture and mix to combine.
7. Gently fold in the egg whites.
8. Transfer the mixture into the prepared pan evenly and top with the plums, skin side down, attractively.
9. Cook in the oven for about 40 minutes or till a toothpick inserted in the center comes out clean.
10. Remove from the oven and cool for about 10 minutes before turning out onto wire rack to cool completely.

Traditional French Dessert

 Prep Time: 10 mins
 Total Time: 1 hr 10 mins

Servings per Recipe: 8
Calories	186 kcal
Fat	3.1 g
Carbohydrates	34.9g
Protein	5.6 g
Cholesterol	73 mg
Sodium	63 mg

Ingredients

- 6 tbsp white sugar, divided
- 14 Italian prune plums, halved and pitted
- 3 eggs
- 1 1/3 C. milk
- 2/3 C. all-purpose flour
- 1 1/2 tsp grated lemon zest
- 2 tsp vanilla
- 1 pinch salt
- 1/2 tsp ground cinnamon
- 2 tbsp confectioners' sugar

Directions

1. Set your oven to 375 degrees F before doing anything else and butter a 10-inch pie plate, then sprinkle 1 tbsp of the sugar over the bottom.
2. In the bottom of the prepared pan, place the plum halves evenly, cut side down and sprinkle with 2 tbsp of the sugar.
3. In a blender, add the remaining 3 tbsp of the sugar, eggs, milk, flour, lemon zest, cinnamon, vanilla and salt and pulse till smooth.
4. Place the pureed mixture over the plum evenly.
5. Cook in the oven for about 50-60 minute.
6. Remove from the oven and keep aside for about 5 minutes before slicing.
7. Dust with the confectioner's sugar before serving.

JALAPENO Plum Chipotle Sauce

🥣 Prep Time: 1 hr
🕒 Total Time: 4 hrs 40 mins

Servings per Recipe: 128
Calories   50 kcal
Fat   0.1 g
Carbohydrates   12.5g
Protein   0.2 g
Cholesterol   0 mg
Sodium   179 mg

Ingredients

5 quarts very ripe plums, pitted
4 cloves garlic, pressed
1 onion, finely chopped
6 C. white sugar
2 tbsp Southwest chipotle seasoning
1 tbsp roasted garlic seasoning
1 jalapeno pepper, finely chopped (remove seeds for milder flavor if desired)
1/2 C. apple cider vinegar
7 tsp salt
1 tsp liquid smoke flavoring (optional)
8 half-pint canning jars with lids and rings

Directions

1. Arrange a colander over a large bowl.
2. Place the plums in the colander and with gloved hands, squeeze the plums in the colander, forcing the juice through the holes of the colander.
3. Discard the spent pulp, and repeat to produce 8 C. of the plum juice.
4. In a small pan, add 3/4 C. of the plum juice, garlic and onion on medium heat and bring to a boil.
5. Reduce the heat to medium-low and simmer for about 5 minutes.
6. In a large pan, add the juice-onion mixture with the remaining 7 1/2 C. of plum juice, sugar, apple cider vinegar, Southwest chipotle seasoning, roasted garlic seasoning, jalapeño pepper, salt and liquid smoke flavoring and stir till the sugar is dissolved.
7. Bring to a boil on medium heat.
8. Reduce heat to a simmer and cook for about 1 1/2 hours, stirring occasionally.
9. Sterilize the jars and lids in boiling water for at least 5 minutes.
10. Place the sauce into the hot, sterilized jars, filling the jars to within 1/4-inch of the top.

11. Run a knife around the insides of the jars to remove any air bubbles.
12. With a moist paper towel, wipe the rims of the jars to remove any food residue.
13. Top with the lids and screw on rings.
14. Place a rack in the bottom of a large pan and fill halfway with the water.
15. Bring to a boil on high heat.
16. With a holder carefully, lower the jars into the pan, leaving a 2-inch space between the jars.
17. Bring the water to a full boil and process, covered for about 10 minutes.
18. Remove the jars from the pan and place onto a wood surface, several inches apart to cool.
19. After cooling, press the top of each lid with a finger, ensuring that the seal is tight.
20. Store in a cool, dark area.

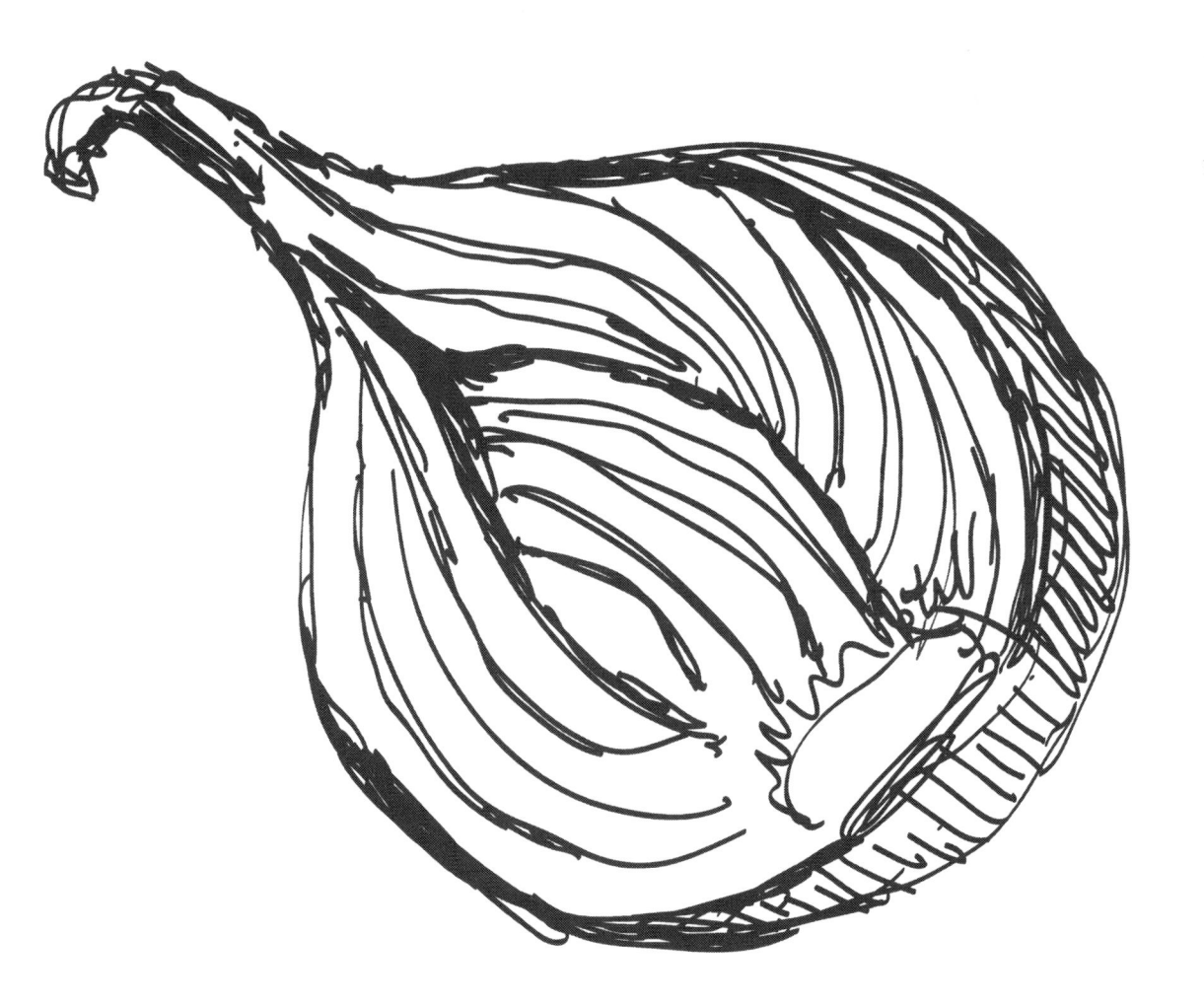

PERSIAN INSPIRED
Cardamom and Plum Jam

🥣 Prep Time: 5 hrs 30 mins
🕒 Total Time: 7 hrs 30 mins

Servings per Recipe: 100
Calories   42 kcal
Fat   0.1 g
Carbohydrates   10.7g
Protein   0.2 g
Cholesterol   1 mg
Sodium   1 mg

Ingredients

5 lb. fresh Damask plums
1 C. water
12 whole cardamom pods
4 C. white sugar
1/4 tsp butter

Directions

1. Rinse the plum and remove the stems.
2. In a thick-bottomed and deep pan, add the plums, water and cardamom pods and bring them to a gentle boil on medium heat.
3. Reduce the heat to low and simmer, uncovered for about 1 1/2 hours.
4. Remove from the heat and keep aside to cool.
5. Place the plums in a colander and with your hands, press the cooled plums to extract the juice in a large bowl.
6. Pick up the pit-and-fruit slurry in the colander by small handfuls and squeeze the plum pulp and skins gently into the bowl with the syrup.
7. Return the plum juice in the pan with the sugar and butter on very low heat.
8. Simmer for about 4 hours.
9. Place the hot jam into hot, sterile jars.
10. Wipe the rims clean and place sterile lids on, then tighten the screw caps.
11. Keep the jars in room temperature to cool.

New Age Plum Cake

🍲 Prep Time: 30 mins
🕐 Total Time: 1 hr 20 mins

Servings per Recipe: 8
Calories	264 kcal
Fat	13 g
Carbohydrates	35g
Protein	3.7 g
Cholesterol	77 mg
Sodium	306 mg

Ingredients

- 1/2 C. whole wheat flour
- 1/2 C. all-purpose flour
- 1 tsp baking powder
- 1/2 tsp salt
- 1/2 C. butter, softened
- 3/4 C. white sugar
- 2 eggs
- 3 plums, pitted and sliced
- 1 tbsp white sugar
- 1 tsp cinnamon

Directions

1. Set your oven to 350 degrees F before doing anything else and grease an 11x7-inch baking dish.
2. In a bowl, mix together the whole wheat flour, white flour, baking powder and salt.
3. In another large bowl, add the butter and 3/4 C. of the sugar and beat till creamy.
4. Add the eggs, one at a time, beating till well combined.
5. Add the flour mixture into the egg mixture and gently, mix till just combined.
6. Transfer the mixture into the prepared baking dish and with the sliced plums.
7. Sprinkle 1 tbsp sugar and cinnamon over the plums.
8. Cook in the oven for about 50-55 minutes or till a toothpick inserted in the center comes out clean.

AGAVE
Butter

🍲 Prep Time: 15 mins
🕐 Total Time: 2 hrs

Servings per Recipe: 40
Calories   50 kcal
Fat   0.2 g
Carbohydrates   13g
Protein   0.2 g
Cholesterol   0 mg
Sodium   1 mg

Ingredients

2 lb. plums, pitted and sliced
2 lb. apples - peeled, cored, and chopped
1 C. apple juice
1 C. agave nectar

1 1/2 tsp ground cinnamon
1 tsp ground cloves
1 tsp ground allspice
1 tsp ground ginger

Directions

1. In a large pan, mix together the plums, apples and apple juice on medium heat and simmer, covered for about 15 minutes.
2. With a potato masher, mash the fruit.
3. Stir in the agave nectar, cinnamon, cloves, allspice and ginger and simmer for about 30-50 minutes, stirring occasionally.
4. Remove from heat and keep aside for at least 1 hour to cool completely.
5. Place the apple butter into jars and cover with a lid.
6. Refrigerate for up to 3 weeks or freeze for up to 6 months.

Fruity Plum Rolls German Style

Prep Time: 40 mins
Total Time: 1 hr 30 mins

Servings per Recipe: 12
Calories	499 kcal
Fat	24.9 g
Carbohydrates	62.7g
Protein	8.8 g
Cholesterol	34 mg
Sodium	618 mg

Ingredients

- 1 C. chopped almonds
- 1 1/3 C. cream cheese
- 1/2 C. milk
- 1/2 C. vegetable oil
- 1 pinch salt
- 5/8 C. white sugar
- 1 tsp ground cinnamon
- 4 C. all-purpose flour
- 1/4 C. baking powder
- 7/8 C. plum butter
- 1 3/4 lb. plums, pitted and diced
- 2 tbsp butter, melted

Directions

1. Set your oven to 350 degrees F before doing anything else and grease a 10-inch spring form pan.
2. Heat a skillet on medium-high heat and toast the almonds till browned.
3. Remove from heat and keep aside to cool.
4. In a bowl, add the cream cheese, milk, oil, salt, sugar and cinnamon and beat till well combined.
5. Add the flour and baking powder and knead the mixture till smooth.
6. Place the dough onto a lightly floured surface and roll into a 20-inch square.
7. Spread the plum butter, plums, and toasted almonds over the dough and roll tightly like a jelly roll.
8. Cut the dough roll into 12 equal sized slices.
9. Place the rolls in the prepared pan in a single layer and coat the top of each roll with the butter.
10. Cook in the oven for about 40-55 minutes.

PLUM
Poblano Salsa

🥣 Prep Time: 15 mins
🕐 Total Time: 1 hr 15 mins

Servings per Recipe: 12
Calories   20 kcal
Fat   0.2 g
Carbohydrates   4.6g
Protein   0.6 g
Cholesterol   0 mg
Sodium   101 mg

Ingredients

2 large tomatoes, diced
1/2 small red onion, diced
4 plums, pitted and diced
1 Poblano chili pepper, seeded and finely chopped
8 sprigs fresh cilantro, chopped (optional)
1 tsp minced garlic
1 tsp lime juice
1/2 tsp salt
1/4 tsp freshly ground black pepper
1/4 tsp chili powder

Directions

1. In a large bowl, mix together the tomatoes, onion, plums, Poblano chili pepper, cilantro, garlic, lime juice, salt, black pepper and chili powder.
2. With a plastic wrap, cover the bowl and refrigerate for at least 1 hour.

Plum No Sugar Butter

Prep Time: 10 mins
Total Time: 2 hrs 25 mins

Servings per Recipe: 16
Calories   10 kcal
Fat   0 g
Carbohydrates   2.4g
Protein   0.1 g
Cholesterol   0 mg
Sodium   1 mg

Ingredients

- 1 C. finely chopped, peeled peaches
- 1 C. pitted, chopped plums
- 1 tbsp water
- 1/2 tsp ground cinnamon
- 1/2 tsp ground ginger
- 1/2 C. granular no-calorie sucralose sweetener (such as Splenda(R))

Directions

1. In a microwave-safe glass bowl, mix together the peaches, plums and water and microwave on high for about 15 minutes, stirring after every 3 minutes.
2. Stir in the cinnamon, ginger and sweetener.
3. Place the fruit butter into a jar and refrigerate, covered before serving.

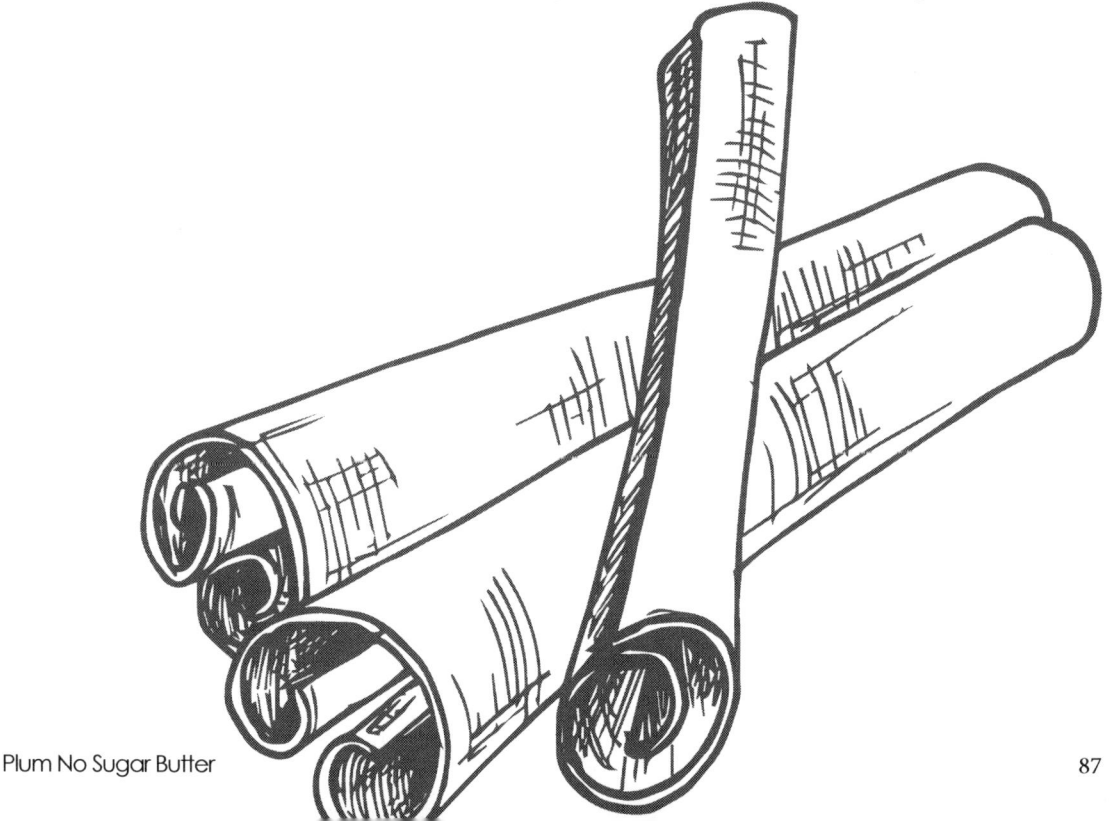

ASIAN INSPIRED
Chicken

🥣 Prep Time: 10 mins
🕐 Total Time: 50 mins

Servings per Recipe: 4
Calories   496 kcal
Fat   21.1 g
Carbohydrates   37.6 g
Protein   37.9 g
Cholesterol   120 mg
Sodium   217 mg

Ingredients

1 (2.5 lb.) whole chicken, cut into pieces
salt and ground black pepper to taste
2/3 C. plum jam
1 1/2 tsp ground black pepper
1 1/2 tsp minced fresh ginger root
1 1/4 tsp prepared horseradish (optional)

Directions

1. Set your oven to 350 degrees F before doing anything else and grease a baking sheet.
2. Season the chicken pieces with the salt and pepper.
3. In the prepared baking sheet, place the chicken, skin-side-up.
4. Cook in the oven for about 20 minutes.
5. Meanwhile in a bowl, mix together the plum jam, 1 1/2 tsp of the pepper, ginger and horseradish.
6. Remove the chicken from the oven and coat the plum glaze.
7. Cook in the oven for about 20-30 minutes more.

I ♥ Strawberry Drinks

🥣 Prep Time: 5 mins
🕐 Total Time: 5 mins

Servings per Recipe: 2
Calories   161.8
Fat   2.4g
Cholesterol   8.5mg
Sodium   32.7mg
Carbohydrates   33.4g
Protein   2.4g

Ingredients

1 C. strawberry, sliced
1/2 C. milk
1/2 C. water
1/4 C. caster sugar

1/2-2/3 tsp vanilla

Directions

1. Slice up enough fresh strawberries to fill one cup.
2. In a food processor, add strawberries and remaining Ingredients and pulse till smooth.

STRAWBERRY
Shortcake 101

🥣 Prep Time: 20 mins
🕐 Total Time: 20 mins

Servings per Recipe: 12
Calories   296.8
Fat   11.5g
Cholesterol   20.8mg
Sodium   235.3mg
Carbohydrates   46.5g
Protein   3.7g

Ingredients

1 quart fresh strawberries
1/2 C. sugar
8 oz. cream cheese, softened
1 (8 oz.) containers frozen whipped topping
1 C. powdered sugar
1 (14 oz.) angel food cake, cut into cubes

Directions

1. Wash, stem and halve the strawberries.
2. In a bowl, add the strawberries and sugar and toss to coat well.
3. Refrigerate to chill.
4. In another bowl, add the cream cheese and powdered sugar and beat well.
5. Fold in the whipped topping and cake cubes.
6. Place the cake into an ungreased 13x9-inch baking dish.
7. Refrigerate, covered for at least 2 hours.
8. Cut the chilled cake into squares and serve with the topping of the strawberries.

Bread for Brunch

🥣 Prep Time: 15 mins
🕐 Total Time: 1 hr 15 mins

Servings per Recipe: 10
Calories   283.7
Fat   12.7g
Cholesterol   67.5mg
Sodium   272.6mg
Carbohydrates   39.0g
Protein   3.9g

Ingredients

1 3/4 C. flour
1/2 tsp baking powder
1/4 tsp baking soda
1/2 tsp salt
1/4 tsp cinnamon
1/2 C. butter, softened
3/4 C. sugar
1/4 C. light brown sugar
2 eggs, room temperature
1/2 C. sour cream, room temperature
1 tsp vanilla
1 1/4 C. strawberries, fresh & coarsely chopped
3/4 C. walnuts (optional)

Directions

1. Set your oven to 350 degrees F before doing anything else and grease an 8x4-inch loaf pan.
2. In a large bowl, mix together the flour, baking powder, baking soda, salt and cinnamon and keep aside.
3. In small bowl, add the butter and beat till creamy.
4. Slowly, add the sugar, beating continuously till light and airy.
5. Add the brown sugar and mix well.
6. Add the eggs, one at a time, beating continuously till well combined.
7. Add the sour cream and vanilla and beat till well combined.
8. Add the flour mixture and mix till just moistened.
9. Fold in the strawberries and walnuts.
10. Transfer the mixture into the prepared loaf pan.
11. Cook in the oven for about 60-65 minutes.
12. Remove from the oven and keep onto wire rack for about 10 minutes.
13. Carefully, invert the cakes onto wire rack to cool completely.

WEEKEND
Breakfast Muffins

🍲 Prep Time: 10 mins
🕒 Total Time: 35 mins

Servings per Recipe: 1
Calories   242.6
Fat   9.0g
Cholesterol   52.7mg
Sodium   297.1mg
Carbohydrates   37.1g
Protein   3.7g

Ingredients

2 C. flour
2 tbsp baking powder
1/2 tsp salt
1 C. sugar
6 tsp sugar
1 1/2 C. chopped strawberries
2 eggs
1/2-1 C. unsalted butter, melted

1/2 C. milk
1 tsp vanilla extract

Directions

1. Set your oven to 375 degrees F before doing anything else and line the cups of muffin pans with the paper liners.
2. In a large bowl, mix together the flour, baking powder, salt and 1 C. of the sugar.
3. Add the strawberries and toss to coat well.
4. In another bowl, add the eggs, butter, milk and vanilla and beat till well combined.
5. Add the egg mixture Ingredients to the flour mixture and mix till just combined.
6. Transfer the mixture into the prepared muffin cups evenly and sprinkle with 1/2 tsp of the sugar evenly.
7. Cook in the oven for about 25 minutes or till a toothpick inserted in the center comes out clean.

John the Juice Smoothie

🥣 Prep Time: 5 mins
🕐 Total Time: 5 mins

Servings per Recipe: 1
Calories   168.4
Fat   6.1g
Cholesterol   22.7mg
Sodium   83.6mg
Carbohydrates   23.8g
Protein   5.7g

Ingredients

1 1/2 C. milk
1 C. strawberry
2 tbsp sugar
1 tsp lemon juice

1 C. crushed ice

Directions

1. In a blender, add all the Ingredients and pulse till smooth.

ALTERNATIVE
Jam

🥣 Prep Time: 5 mins
🕐 Total Time: 5 mins

Servings per Recipe: 1
Calories　　　　578.4
Fat　　　　　　1.0g
Cholesterol　　　0.0mg
Sodium　　　　6.4mg
Carbohydrates　145.8g
Protein　　　　2.4g

Ingredients

2 1/2 C. coarsely chopped hulled strawberries
1/2 C. sugar

2 1/2 tbsp cornstarch

Directions

1. In a heavy small pan, add all the Ingredients and bring to a boil, crushing the berries slightly with the back of spoon.
2. Now, boil for about 2 minutes, stirring continuously.
3. Transfer the mixture into a bowl and refrigerate to cool completely.

Northern California Lemonade

Prep Time: 10 mins
Total Time: 10 mins

Servings per Recipe: 8
Calories   100.6
Fat   0.2g
Cholesterol   0.0mg
Sodium   16.2mg
Carbohydrates   25.8g
Protein   0.5g

Ingredients

3 C. water, cold
1 quart fresh strawberries
3/4 C. sugar
3/4 C. lemon juice

2 C. club soda, cold
Lemon slice (optional)

Directions

1. In a blender, add the water, strawberries and sugar and pulse till smooth.
2. Add the lemon juice and soda and pulse till combined.
3. Serve immediately with a garnishing of the lemon slices.

5-INGREDIENT Cinnamon Strawberry Crisp

Prep Time: 10 mins
Total Time: 25 mins

Servings per Recipe: 2
Calories   256.8
Fat   7.3g
Cholesterol   15.2mg
Sodium   60.3mg
Carbohydrates   46.7g
Protein   3.2g

Ingredients

1 tbsp butter
1/2 C. uncooked oatmeal
1/4 C. packed brown sugar
1/2 tsp cinnamon

1 C. sliced strawberry

Directions

1. Set your oven to 375 degrees F before doing anything else.
2. In a small pan, melt the butter on low heat.
3. Add the oatmeal, brown sugar and cinnamon and mix well.
4. Immediately, remove from the heat.
5. Place the strawberries in 2 oven-proof dishes evenly and top with the oatmeal mixture.
6. Cook in the oven for about 15 minutes.

Perfect Strawberry Topping

Prep Time: 10 mins
Total Time: 20 mins

Servings per Recipe: 12
Calories   58.6
Fat   0.2g
Cholesterol   0.0mg
Sodium   13.8mg
Carbohydrates   14.7g
Protein   0.5g

Ingredients

2 lb. ripe strawberries, hulled
1/2 C. granulated sugar
2 tsp cornstarch
1/2 lemon, juice of
1 pinch salt

Directions

1. In a medium pan, mix together all the Ingredients on medium-low heat and cook for about 10 minutes, stirring gently.
2. Remove from heat and keep aside to cool.

ZANZIBAR Pie

🥣 Prep Time: 10 mins
🕐 Total Time: 40 mins

Servings per Recipe: 6
Calories   343.4
Fat   10.3g
Cholesterol   98.0mg
Sodium   308.6mg
Carbohydrates   58.7g
Protein   5.4g

Ingredients

3 eggs, beaten
2 1/2 C. rhubarb, red, 1 inch slices
1 1/4 C. sugar
1 1/2 C. strawberries, fresh, sliced
1/4 C. enriched flour
1 9" pastry crust with lattice top
1/4 tsp salt
1 tbsp butter

1/2 tsp allspice
Whole strawberries, as required

Directions

1. Set your oven to 400 degrees F before doing anything else.
2. In a large bowl, add the eggs, sugar, flour, salt and allspice and mix well.
3. In another bowl, mix together the rhubarb and sliced strawberries.
4. Arrange the pastry crust into a 9-inch pie dish.
5. Place the strawberry mixture over the crust evenly and top with the egg mixture evenly.
6. Place the butter on top in the form of dots.
7. Arrange the lattice crust on top, crimping the edge high.
8. Cook in the oven for about 40 minutes.
9. Fill the openings of the lattice crust with whole strawberries.
10. Serve warm.

Lunch Box Salad

Prep Time: 3 mins
Total Time: 45 mins

Servings per Recipe: 18
Calories   345.4
Fat   15.9 g
Cholesterol   34.2 mg
Sodium   499.3 mg
Carbohydrates   48.2 g
Protein   4.4 g

Ingredients

- 2 C. crushed pretzels
- 3/4 C. butter, melted
- 3 tbsp white sugar
- 1 (8 oz.) packages cream cheese, softened
- 1 C. white sugar
- 1 (8 oz.) cartons frozen whipped topping, thawed
- 2 (3 oz.) packages strawberry gelatin
- 2 C. boiling water
- 2 (10 oz.) packages frozen strawberries

Directions

1. Set your oven to 400 degrees F before doing anything else.
2. In a bowl, add the crushed pretzels, melted butter and 3 tbsp of the white sugar and mix till well combined.
3. In the bottom of 13x9-inch baking dish, place the pretzel mixture and press to smooth the surface.
4. Cook in the oven for about 8-10 minutes.
5. Remove from the oven and keep aside to cool.
6. In a large bowl, add the cream cheese and white sugar and beat till creamy.
7. Fold in the whipped topping.
8. Place the cream cheese mixture over the cooled crust.
9. In a bowl of the boiling water, dissolve the gelatin.
10. Stir in the frozen strawberries and keep aside to set slightly.
11. Place the strawberry mixture over the cream cheese mixture evenly.
12. Refrigerate till set completely.

ARTISANAL
Syrup

🥣 Prep Time: 10 mins
🕐 Total Time: 15 mins

Servings per Recipe: 1
Calories	738.9
Fat	0.4g
Cholesterol	0.0mg
Sodium	3.3mg
Carbohydrates	189.9g
Protein	1.0g

Ingredients

1 pint fresh strawberries
2 C. sugar
1/4 tsp lemon juice

Directions

1. In a food processor, add the strawberries and pulse till smooth.
2. Through a wire-mesh strainer, strain the strawberry puree into a pan
3. Discard the seeds.
4. In the pan, add the sugar and juice on low heat and cook till the sugar dissolves, stirring continuously.
5. Increase the heat to medium-high and bring to a boil.
6. Reduce the heat and simmer for about 5 minutes, skimming the froth from the top.
7. Remove from the heat and keep aside to cool.

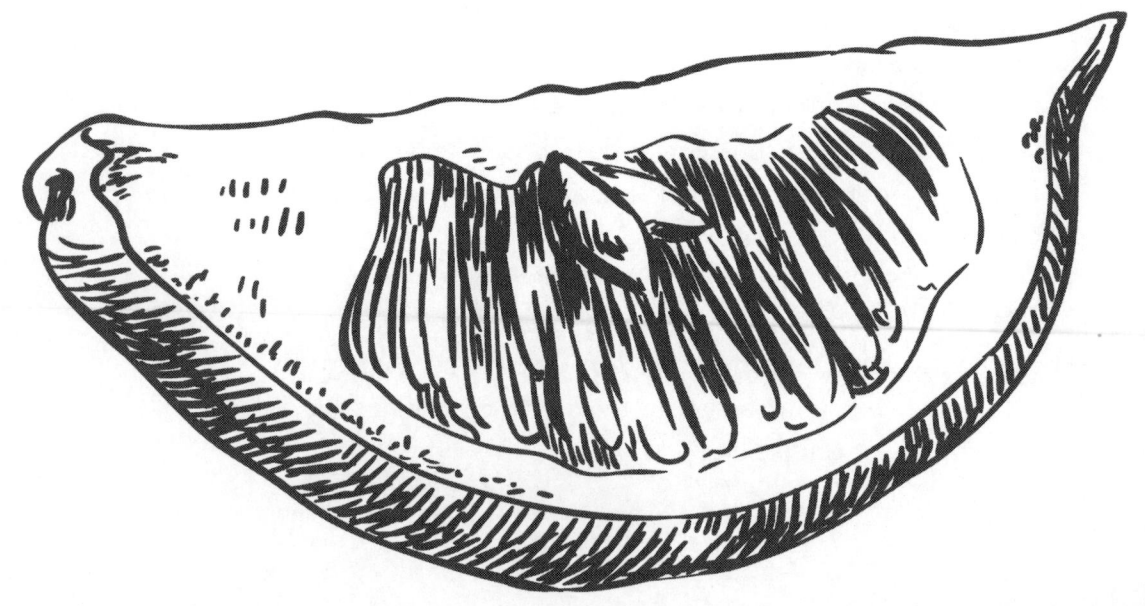

Fruity Nachos

⏲ Prep Time: 1 hr 30 mins
🕐 Total Time: 1 hr 38 mins

Servings per Recipe: 6
Calories	284.3
Fat	14.0g
Cholesterol	22.8mg
Sodium	234.4mg
Carbohydrates	37.0g
Protein	4.5g

Ingredients

3 C. sliced fresh strawberries
1/4 C. sugar
1/4 C. almond flavored liqueur (such as Amaretto)
3/4 C. sour cream
2 tbsp sugar
1/4 tsp cinnamon

6 6-inch flour tortillas
2 tbsp melted butter
2 tsp sugar
1/4 tsp cinnamon
2 tbsp sliced almonds, toasted
1 tbsp shaved semisweet chocolate

Directions

1. In a bowl, add the strawberries, 1/4 C. of the sugar and almond-flavored liqueur and mix well.
2. Refrigerate, covered for at least 1 hour.
3. In another bowl, add the sour cream, 2 tbsp of the sugar and 1/4 tsp of the cinnamon and mix till well combined.
4. Refrigerate, covered till using.
5. Set your oven to 400 degrees F.
6. With a pastry brush, lightly coat 1 side of the tortillas with the melted butter.
7. Cut each tortilla into 6 equal sized wedges.
8. Place the tortilla wedges onto 2 ungreased baking sheets in a single layer and sprinkle with 2 tsp of the sugar and 1/4 tsp of the cinnamon.
9. Cook in the oven for about 6-8 minutes.
10. Remove from the oven and keep aside to cool.
11. Remove the strawberries from the refrigerator and drain completely.
12. Divide the tortilla wedges into 6 dessert bowls and top with the strawberries and a little of the sour cream mixture.
13. Serve with a topping of the toasted almonds and shaved chocolate.

MEDITERRANEAN
Strawberries

🥣 Prep Time: 15 mins
🕐 Total Time: 2 hrs 15 mins

Servings per Recipe: 6
Calories 39.9
Fat 0.1g
Cholesterol 0.0mg
Sodium 1.8mg
Carbohydrates 9.6g
Protein 0.4g

Ingredients

1 pint ripe strawberry
2 tbsp sugar
2 tbsp balsamic vinegar

Directions

1. Hull the strawberries and cut into quarters lengthwise.
2. In a bowl, add the strawberries, vinegar and sugar and toss to coat well.
3. Cover the bowl and keep aside for about 1 hour.
4. Now, refrigerate to chill for about 1 hour.
5. Remove from the refrigerator and toss again before serving.

Strawberry Smoothie Bowl

Prep Time: 15 mins
Total Time: 15 mins

Servings per Recipe: 8
Calories   127.2
Fat   5.7g
Cholesterol   20.3mg
Sodium   20.2mg
Carbohydrates   18.4g
Protein   1.6g

Ingredients

500 g strawberries, hulled
2 large egg whites, at room temperature
1/2 C. caster sugar
1/2 C. whipping cream
1/4-1/2 tsp vanilla
6 -8 strawberries, sliced, for garnish
Mint leaf

Directions

1. In a blender, add the strawberries and pulse till smooth.
2. In a bowl, add the strawberry puree, egg whites and sugar and beat till stiff and glossy.
3. In another bowl, add the cream and vanilla and beat till peaks form.
4. Gently fold the cream mixture into the strawberry mixture.
5. Transfer the mixture into a serving bowl and top with the strawberry slices and mint.
6. With a plastic wrap, cover the bowl and refrigerate before serving.

SPRING
Sorbet 101

🥣 Prep Time: 20 mins
🕐 Total Time: 2 hrs 20 mins

Servings per Recipe: 6
Calories   125.0
Fat   0.2g
Cholesterol   0.0mg
Sodium   1.5mg
Carbohydrates   31.7g
Protein   0.5g

Ingredients

1 C. water
3/4 C. sugar
1 pint fresh strawberries

1/2 C. orange juice

Directions

1. Combine water & sugar in a pan, stir over low heat until sugar dissolves.
2. Bring to a boil & boil gently for 5 minutes without stirring.
3. Set aside to cool.
4. Wash berries.
5. Remove caps.
6. Puree fruit in a blender or food processor until almost smooth.
7. In a medium bowl, combine fruit with cooled syrup and orange juice.
8. If you have an ice cream freezer, you can put the puree mixture into that & process using the directions
9. In a pan, add the water and sugar on low heat and cook till the sugar dissolves, stirring continuously.
10. Bring to a boil and then boil for about 5 minutes without stirring.
11. Remove from the heat and keep aside to cool.
12. Wash the strawberries and hull them.
13. In a blender, add the strawberries and pulse till smooth.
14. In a bowl, mix together the strawberry puree, cooled sugar syrup and orange juice.
15. Transfer the mixture into ice cream maker and process according to manufacturers

Printed in Great Britain
by Amazon

9fa027cb-9311-46e2-82ea-cdc776151483R01